"The Christian perspective on the human past must be judged by the validity of Christianity itself. If the Christian faith is a tissue of myths, it can only provide a mythological view of the past. But if the Bible is true, and if Jesus Christ is really 'the way, and the truth, and the life' as he claims, then the Christian's view of the past will be the clearest of all."

HISTORY
in the Making

An Introduction
to the Study of
the Past

Roy Swanstrom

InterVarsity Press
Downers Grove
Illinois 60515

InterVarsity Press is the book-publishing
division of Inter-Varsity Christian
Fellowship, a student movement active on
campus at hundreds of universities,
colleges and schools of nursing. For
information about local and regional
activities, write IVCF, 233 Langdon St.,
Madison, WI 53703.

Distributed in Canada through
InterVarsity Press, 1875 Leslie St., Unit 10,
Don Mills, Ontario M3B 2M5, Canada.

All Scripture quotations, unless otherwise
indicated, are from the Revised Standard
Version of the Bible, copyrighted 1946, 1952,
© 1971, 1973.

ISBN 0-87784-581-6
Library of Congress Catalog Card
Number: 78-13881

Printed in the United States of America

History:
What's
the Use?

1

The scene is the registration line at the beginning of the college term.

"My academic adviser wants me to sign up for Western Civilization—says it'll help me develop a historical perspective."

"Negative. I've heard that Professor Edelweiss is a low grader—I don't want to ruin my g.p.a. Besides, ol' Edelpuss loads you up with too much reading. Hard on the eyes—and the brain."

"No history for me, either. My worst subject in high school —bored me stiff with all those names and dates."

"Count me out, too. I'd rather study about the living than the dead. Better to look ahead than to look back."

We history instructors have heard these objections, and scads of others, since our first day behind the podium— sometimes with colorful embellishments. Students are usually too courteous to tell us to our faces that we teach a dead and useless subject, but we have our antennas out and get the message.

Naturally, we are saddened by such attitudes, but we have learned to be philosophical about them. Despite the prevalent notion that history is merely the deadly memorization of forgettable names and dates, we feel in our hearts that ours is the most important subject in the curriculum—for reasons that should become clear as we go along. We like to believe that the student's allergy to history results not from natural perversity but from misapprehensions that can be rectified.

History instructors who are Christians have special reasons for being distressed by negative vibrations about history, particularly among Christian students, because the relationship between history and Christianity is very close. The Christian faith is based squarely on actual historical events. Distinctively Christian insights help us better understand the human past. The study of history greatly enriches our understanding of our faith. At the same time, reflecting on the relationship between Christianity and history raises questions that challenge our deepest intellectual and spiritual discernment.

Some Modest Purposes
This brief introduction to history is addressed specifically to the Christian student enrolled in a college history course, perhaps the first beyond high school. Its purposes are modest. It does not attempt to prove, through history, the validity of our Christian faith. It does not pretend to answer all questions about the relationship between Christianity and historical inquiry. In fact, it may raise, without answering, questions that have not occurred to the student before. Nor does it purport to be a "Christian philosophy of history"; it will only suggest some alternatives that might help the student clarify his own thinking on the subject.

In short, it is not a map that will guide the questioning student through the labyrinthine complexities of history to the shining "Mountain of Truth." This book is more like a travel brochure that suggests how the wayfarer might best profit from a journey through this rich but unfamiliar country. Moreover, it is addressed primarily to students of the Western heritage. While it is hoped that the principles outlined here can be applied to non-Western history, the task of applying them in this manner lies outside the scope of this book.

We will begin with a brief discussion of history as a field of study. Then we will explore some ways in which history and the Christian faith are interrelated—what we mean when we say that Christianity is a "historical religion." Third, we will examine a few alternative answers to questions about the underlying meaning of the human past—some forks in the road where you will have to make up your own mind which direction to go. Fourth, we will summarize some advantages the Christian may enjoy in understanding the past, along with some dangers and pitfalls that must be avoided. Fifth, we will suggest how a study of history can enrich and strengthen our Christian life. Finally, we will introduce some heavy questions involving faith and history.

If the objective in studying history is merely to memorize enough names, dates and other facts to pass a course, earning a few credits toward a degree, the effort will be wearisome and the subject boring. But if we approach history with the realization that it involves real people who hoped and feared and hurt and laughed just as we do; if we recognize their dreams and frustrations, triumphs and tragedies as our own, then history can become as real and vital as life itself. And if we realize that problems people confronted in the long ago and far away are often basically the same issues that confront us today, we might even learn something of inestimable value. Give history a chance. You might even like it.

A Few Matters of Definition

History. How would you define the word *history*? The simplest definition is probably: "History is just one darn thing after another." Gilbert K. Chesterton, a celebrated essayist, said, "History is only a confused heap of facts." Cicero, on the other hand, long ago declared that "history is indeed the witness of the times, the light of truth." The most common definition among college students is matter-of-fact and to the point: "History is the study of the past." This is not strictly correct, for reasons we will discuss. But, obviously, every discussion of history focuses on the past in one way or another. One modern dictionary defines history as "a branch of knowledge that records and explains past events."[1] (Note, for future reference, the word *explains*. And remember that the word *events* here must be interpreted broadly enough to include the expression of ideas and other less tangible occurrences.)

The famous Italian philosopher-historian Benedetto Croce once said that "historical knowledge is not a variety of knowledge, but it is knowledge itself; it is the form which completely fills and exhausts the field of knowing." That takes in quite a bit of territory, perhaps too much. On the other hand, if we know in detail the history of anything or anybody, we know that thing or person rather well. In chapter two we will discuss the scope of history more fully.

A working definition of history is complicated by the fact that in English we sometimes do not distingush between history as the event itself ("World War 2 is history now") and history as the recording of the event ("I'm reading a history of World War 2"). We may begin to limit the subject matter of history somewhat by insisting that we confine the discussion to *significant* occurrences out of the past. The fact that Bodo the peasant (or his lord, for that matter) blew his nose at 4:20 in the afternoon of April 13, 1263, need not be considered a historical event. Also, we may exclude events that happen with clocklike regularity as a matter of course. The fact, for example, that the sun rose in Los Angeles at 5:53 A.M. on July 18, 1944, needs no special notice. (But if the sun had *not* risen that hour, *that* really would have been a historical event.) Historical studies concentrate on occurrences that are both significant and generally unrepeated.

Two Ways of Looking at History. In the Christian community there are two rather different ways of looking at history. The first deals with relatively concrete or specific events and movements of the past. It may involve events of only momentary duration, such as Neil Armstrong stepping out of his spacecraft onto the surface of the moon, or events of longer duration such as the Hundred Years' War or the Industrial Revolution. But in either case it involves human events potentially verifiable through some kind of documentary or archaeological evidence. For our purposes here we might call this "classroom history," because most college history courses confine themselves to this type.

In the other way of looking at history, the basic question is, Does the whole course of human history have any meaning and, if so, what is it? Such a question, obviously, does not lend itself to the usual kind of historical investigation conducted by professional historians. One does not find an answer to this question just by examining and evaluating historical records. In the last analysis the answers do not come out of history itself, but out of the individual's inner convictions or (the Christian believes) from divine revelation. There is sometimes the implication that human events are altered by supernatural forces struggling over the destiny of mankind.

In the Christian context, this kind of history, sometimes referred to as "redemption history" or "salvation history," embraces the heart of the gospel message. In the beginning God created a perfect universe and a sinless man and woman to enjoy fellowship with him in love. The human race fell from this high estate through pride and disobedience, bringing into the world sorrow, suffering and physical and spiritual death. God, however, not frustrated by human failure, began to execute his grand redemptive design. He appointed a chosen people, the Hebrews, through whom he would reveal himself and perpetuate the knowledge of God in the world. Then, in the crucial, climactic event of history, God himself in the person of Jesus Christ became a man, endured without sin all the temptations and woes that afflict the human race, and finally conquered both sin and death through his crucifixion and resurrection. Before his ascension into heaven he ordained his church to preach the gospel to all the world and promised to come again at the close of time to judge the world and establish his eternal kingdom.

You will note that these two kinds of history—"classroom history" and "redemption history"—are in many ways poles apart in both subject matter and implications. College history instructors usually shy away from the second, considering it the province of theologians or philosophers rather than historians. We feel much more at home in the archives, examining documents which may shed new light on some specific event or discussing with students the results of such research.

The types of evidence usually demanded by these two kinds of history are very different. For instance, in ordinary history we can get a fairly good picture of the causes of the American Civil War by examining the public and private papers of perceptive and influential people of that day or the records of popular feeling in the North and South in the prewar period. But what kind of evidence will tell us the purposes of God in creating the world or explain the divine-human nature of Christ?

The line of demarcation between the two kinds of history, however, is not precise. This is due partly to the fact that every historian, regardless of the material he is dealing with, begins with some premises or postulates that are not derived from history itself. Also, the Christian believes that God is sovereign over his eternal purposes beyond the limits of time, as well as over specific, concrete events, both great and small, in recorded history. We must remember, too, that crucial events of "redemption history" took place right here on our planet within recorded time. Christians believe that the central event of all history—the crucifixion of Christ—was the key act in God's eternal strategy for the salvation of mankind and at the same time a concrete event of human history verified by eyewitnesses. Our purpose at this point, however, is not to develop the differing purposes of these two categories of history, but merely to call your attention to the existence of the two kinds and thus to avoid confusion as we continue our discussion.

Because the aim of this volume is to introduce Christian students to college studies in history, it will be concerned primarily with the kind of material usually dealt with in such courses, in other words, with the record of tangible events on this planet. But Christians can hardly avoid thinking about how such events relate to the larger purposes of God in creation and human salvation.

Christian. Since the term *Christian* has traditionally been used loosely and with many different connotations, perhaps before going any further we should define how we will use it here.

For the purposes of our discussion, the word applies to a person who trusts in Christ as Redeemer and Lord, who identifies himself or herself as Christ's follower, who accepts the authority of the Scriptures in thought and conduct, and who endeavors to live a Christ-honoring life. It does not here refer to "culture Christians"—those whose claim to membership in Christ's family is based on their belonging to a so-called Christian community or being subject to Christian influences. On the other hand, we must remember that there are many people who have made no genuine commitment to Christ as Savior and Lord who nevertheless accept some features of the Christian world view.

The term *Christian* implies belief in God as the Creator to whom all are responsible for their acts and purposes. It implies the primacy of the spiritual, since mankind has an eternal destiny beyond the grave. These implications determine the values and priorities we bring to our study of history and have much to say about the meaning of success and failure in human endeavors described in history. *Christian* suggests a specific standard of evaluating people, ideas and movements.

How, when and whether to apply the word *Christian* to a society as a whole also presents problems. There has probably never been a community anywhere that has been completely Christian in the sense of reflecting, in spirit and practice, the standards of Christ. On the other hand, our Western culture since ancient times has been influenced, in greater or lesser degree, by Christians and Christian beliefs and values. This was especially true in the Middle Ages, when Europe, in spite of many unchristian practices and much misunderstanding of the essentials of the Christian faith, was often referred to as "Christendom." Even today, Western civilization is influenced more strongly by its Christian legacy than most people realize.

With these observations in mind, we will take a closer look at history as an academic discipline and as a field of study.

What Is History?

2

Have you ever said to yourself, "Why should I be concerned about the past? It's dead, dead forever." If you have, please reconsider. Are you really so unconcerned about the past? Athletes who would not be caught dead with a history book can give us the won-lost record of every New York Yankee baseball team from the days of Babe Ruth to the present. Majors in fashion design who rank history just a step above warts and acne will go into deliriums of delight reading about the fashions of 1480 or 1795, not realizing that those fashions reflect important aspects of society that interest the stuffy historian. Physics majors who are more at home in the lab than among dry old history books may describe with glowing animation all the events leading up to Kitty Hawk and the first successful aerial flight.

History, History, Everywhere
The fact is, few aspects of the present hold much significance

or can be genuinely understood apart from their historical past. This includes your country, your church denomination, your political party, your school, your service club, your labor union. The list is endless. Even in the realm of thoughts and ideals, few, if any, are really new. Students constantly express surprise that ideas and practices they thought brand new were debated years, perhaps centuries, ago and are what they are today as a result of long historical development.

If you were visiting friends in England and were asked to describe the distinctive characteristics of Americans, how would you reply? Admittedly this is a difficult question and no two Americans would describe their compatriots in just the same way. But if you had thought about the question before, the chances are good that you would mention colonial enterprises, Puritanism, immigration, eighteenth-century political thought, the frontier, the mix of races and cultures, and other aspects of American history. Or if you are English and were asked to describe the uniqueness of the English people, you might start with the Anglo-Saxon and Norman conquests, continue on through the Reformation, the Spanish Armada, overseas expansion and end with the welfare state or the liquidation of the Empire. The more we think about it, the more we realize that the cuffs and buffs of centuries of time have made our societies what they are.

As Christians we may claim, quite sincerely, that all our religious beliefs are derived from the Bible and from nothing else. But this is unlikely. More probably, our beliefs and attitudes have been influenced by events in the history of the church over the past two thousand years, as well as by the social milieu in which we find ourselves, which in turn is the product of historical development. That is why it is necessary to check our beliefs and attitudes from time to time to determine which are essentially and distinctively Christian and which are not.

For the sake of illustration, let us look at the impact of history on an institution with which most of us are rather intimately familiar—our local church.

That church cannot be understood adequately by simply viewing its building, reading its statement of doctrine, attending a service, listening to a sermon or observing its current members. The congregation was founded by people who had certain religious convictions and felt that existing churches did not meet their needs. Why? Who were these people and why did they believe as they did? Over the years various pastors and influential laymen and laywomen left on the church the imprint of their religious convictions and spiritual experiences, not to mention other aspects of their personalities. From time to time crises arose in the congregation which were dealt with in certain ways and left their mark. Outside factors such as wars, economic crises and population movements caused the church to respond in specific ways, which in turn helped shape its personality. It would be an error to think of our local church community as solely the product of historical forces such as these, for we must take into consideration the peculiar and perhaps imponderable work of the Holy Spirit. But even the work of the Holy Spirit was done in a historical context and itself became a part of the church's history. In short, no one can understand the church without careful attention to its historical development.

History Is Human Experience
In my own effort to reduce the complexities of history to manageable proportions, I find it useful to think of history simply in terms of human experience. History does not have some mysterious life of its own. It consists essentially of the composite life and experiences of the people in the society under study. Thus, we do not necessarily have to get involved in great impersonal "laws of historical develop-

ment," but can ask of that society the same kinds of questions we ask concerning individuals. These questions will include inquiry into both the "classroom" and "redemption" types of history.

For example, we could ask to what extent our conduct (yours and mine) has been determined by influences such as heredity, native physical and intellectual endowments, home, school and neighborhood environments, social class, economics and geography, physical drives, and philosophic and religious convictions. What options have been open to us, bearing in mind the perimeters of our talents and discernment? To what extent have our successes and failures been due to our own conscious choices and to what extent to factors beyond our control? Above all, to what extent does God direct our lives? Does he intervene to change their course, perhaps in answer to prayer?

If we can answer such questions we will have gone a long way toward understanding ourselves. And since society consists of other people with natures similar to our own, we will have learned a great deal concerning the forces that make up the fabric of history.

This approach to history is especially significant to us as Christians. We realize that nations and civilizations are under the judgment of God, but that in the last analysis God deals with individuals. The Bible emphasizes that each of us is created in the image of God. What does this say about the intrinsic importance of each actor in the drama of history? Does this not imply that we are not merely the creatures of heredity or environment or chance?

History Is Not a Study of the Past
The beginning student often assumes that the writing of history is rather simple, though perhaps pointless. All one has to do is to get the facts about some past event and then describe it as it actually happened. That is what TV detective

Sergeant Friday did in the old "Dragnet" series when he asked witnesses to "just give us the facts."

But it is not that easy. One big problem is that history is not really a study of the past at all. This is so for the simple but irresistible reason that the past is gone, irretrievably gone, forever. It just is not here to study.

So what do we do? We do the next best thing and study the surviving record of the event. That is why we say that history is not a study of the past but of the *record* of the past. This may seem like first-class quibbling, but the distinction is very important. The biology student can examine a specimen under the microscope. The political scientist can talk to the people immediately involved in the political process. The student of literature can read firsthand the novel or poem under study. But the history student can study only the record of the event, not the event itself.

This might not be an important distinction if that record were complete and accurate or, contrariwise, not hopelessly voluminous. But conditions for research are usually far from ideal. Sound scholarship forces us to look at some serious problems in this area.

The Historian at Work
As we begin to consider these difficulties, let's take a brief look at the way history books are written. First of all, there are several different types of historical works.

Primary Accounts. One type is called a *primary* account because it is a narrative of historical events written by a person who actually participated in them or at least viewed them firsthand. Villehardouin's *Chronicle of the Fourth Crusade* and Alexander Kerensky's description of the Provisional Government he headed before the 1917 Bolshevik Revolution in Russia are two examples. Of course, the historian usually does not have available complete accounts written by eyewitnesses. More likely the narrative must be pieced together from fragmentary material, such as letters, diaries, speeches, reports, business records or whatever else the researcher can find.

Primary sources obviously have very great value, since no one knows better than a participant or immediate observer what actually happened. On the other hand, they also present problems of bias and balance and the vagaries of memory. Six observers of an assassination may give six different descriptions of the event. Even more tricky is a primary account that has been written to vindicate the actions of the writer. This sometimes happens, especially when the actions have been subject to severe criticism. Napoleon Bonaparte's memoirs, written on lonely St. Helena after his final defeat at Waterloo, are an example. Such accounts need to be supplemented by others in order to obtain a fair and objective picture.

Secondary Accounts. Most history books, of course, were not written by participants of the events described, but were penned long afterwards by persons who had no first-hand knowledge of what happened. We can divide such works into two categories—monographs and more general works. (The dividing line between the two categories is not very sharp.) Both involve the problem of sources.

A monograph deals with a limited subject, such as medieval chivalry, the Nazi youth movement, the campaign for woman suffrage, the organization of the Roman army or the Battle of Britain. For obvious reasons, a scholar preparing to write such a work prefers to use, if possible, primary sources. These will be supplemented by material produced by associates of the participants or other contemporaries who had access to pertinent information, as well as by a wide range of other relevant material. In other words, the author of a monograph tries to get as close to the actual event as possible. Note again the crucial importance of valid sources.

The other type of secondary history, more general works,

involves broader topics such as the history of Medieval Europe, of the United States, of the Far East in the modern world and so on. The scholar who writes such a historical work finds it physically impossible to base his or her entire work on primary sources. Even assuming the inquirer has the language skills and other tools to locate, study and evaluate all the pertinent firsthand or contemporary records, it would be far too time consuming. The scholar uses primary records as far as possible, particularly in his own area of specialization. But then it is part of the historian's task to synthesize the work of other scholars, utilizing monographs written by experts in the various topics included in the broader history, adding insights and conclusions of his own. You will probably find a bibliography of such pertinent specialized accounts in the back of your history textbook.

You probably noticed that the author of a historical work of broad scope is usually an additional step removed from the primary sources, but in no sense is less dependent on them. Historical accuracy still depends in large part on the character of these sources. So let's take a closer look at these primary accounts.

The Raw Materials of History
Primary records, the raw materials of history, take innumerable forms: government documents (now in huge quantities and varieties), records of business firms, contemporary newspapers and trade journals, private correspondence, diaries and memoirs, inscriptions on ancient monuments or references in imaginative literature. The list can go on and on. Records need not be written. Much can be learned about ancient history, for example, from architectural remains and all kinds of artifacts dug up by archaeologists. Recent history can be studied from tapes and actual conversations with participants. The historian finds the task of locating pertinent records a fascinating game. It can also be frustrating, though,

since records may be elusive or nonexistent.

Not Enough Records.   A source of particular frustration is the *absence* of pertinent records. The conscientious historian searches everywhere—in damp cellars and musty attics, in rows and rows of filing cabinets, in faded and long-forgotten packets of letters, in thousands of newspaper columns —but relevant facts may still elude him. Very often the actors in the historical drama had no idea that later generations would be interested in what they were doing, and consequently left few if any records of their activities. As a result, there are serious gaps in our knowledge of the past.

We wonder, apparently in vain, when and how and why the first Indians came to the American continents. We know that Leif Ericsson landed on the shores of North America nearly five hundred years before Columbus, but the details of his voyages are shrouded in legend. It is entirely possible that other Europeans preceded Leif the Lucky to America, but we will probably never know for sure. The existence of entire peoples is concealed in mystery. We may never learn what went on behind the closed doors of chancelleries, royal chambers or military command headquarters, or in the "smoke-filled rooms" where political decisions are said to have been made.

When preparing a history of the early days of the United States Senate, I was completely baffled in my search of the records for some mention of the seating arrangement in the Senate chamber. Did the Federalists sit on one side, their opponents on the other? Or was the seating in alphabetical order? Or did the Northerners sit on one side, the senators from the middle states in the middle, and the Southerners on the other side? Or did the members sit where they pleased? This question is probably not of earthshaking importance, although seating arrangements could well have influenced the conduct of business. What was most frustrating was the thought that all the senators whose memoirs and correspondence I consulted knew the answer to my question but not one of them happened to mention the point.

Lack of Proportion. Another glaring defect of primary historical records is that they completely lack proportion. For example, the role of women in history has been sadly neglected and underestimated. This may be due as much to inadequate information as to male chauvinism. For example, we often do not know the extent to which wives, mothers or daughters of kings, generals or presidents affected their decisions. The influence may have been tacit—such as the role that a mother plays in forming her child's values—or it may have been explicit. How many men have received credit for wisdom and energy when actually their wives were the dynamic force? Though at times it may have been quite decisive, the influence of women, especially women of the distant past, has far too often been unrecorded.

Furthermore, the rich, the prominent, the well born and the literate often left voluminous evidence of what they did and thought, while the poor—especially the illiterate—all too frequently lived, endured and died without any recorded evidence that they existed. This should be a matter of special regret for the Christian, whose circle of concern should embrace all people, both great and small.

Winston Churchill, who was a prominent historian and journalist as well as statesman before he became British prime minister in World War 2, was thoroughly aware of the importance of his war leadership to posterity. He kept very careful records of his conduct in office and, after the conflict was over, published *The Second World War,* a work of six large volumes. Naturally and justifiably, it features prominently the prime minister's role in the Allied victory. No criticism of Churchill's writing is implied here since it is an admirable piece of work. But we must remember that millions of humbler people suffered or died on battlefields or in slave-labor camps without any opportunity to describe the war from *their* perspective. Our view of the past is partial and distorted and very different from that of Almighty God, who sees all and loves the great and small without partiality.

Very disconcerting to the historian is the absence of reliable information about the *motives* of men and women who have played significant roles in history. We cannot know the inmost thoughts that impelled crusaders and kings, rebels and peasants, authors and priests to do what they did. If we had such pertinent facts, we might have to revise radically our judgments concerning both the heroes and villains of history. In the meantime, we need to be restrained in our judgments and cultivate the Christian grace of humility in the face of all we do not know about the people of the past.

Unreliable Records.   To complicate matters further, when historians do find pertinent records, they often find them unreliable, due to inadvertent or deliberate error. The author of a contemporary account may have been misinformed or perhaps had some personal motive for deceiving or concealing. When we read a speech in the *Congressional Record* of today, we naturally and correctly assume that the speaker gives only his own side of the question at issue. People were no different in 300 B.C. or A.D. 1884.

In 1830 among the ruins of ancient Nineveh was found a cylinder (the so-called Taylor prism) on which King Sennacherib of Assyria had inscribed an account of his victories over King Hezekiah of Judah. No mention is made of the destruction of the Assyrian army at Jerusalem described in the Bible (2 Kings 19). This could be accepted as proof that this Assyrian catastrophe never occurred and that the biblical account is false. But the alert historian would not consider such an omission conclusive, since it was typical of royal despots to omit from their inscriptions mention of any event which might detract from the glory of their reigns.

There are many manuals designed to aid the fledgling scholar to evaluate the accuracy and objectivity of historical sources. Most of them are very helpful, though none can cover the problems posed by every piece of source material. The principal requirement in making such evaluations is solid common sense. But often special expertise (for example, knowledge of obscure languages, contemporary idioms, social and religious customs and so on) is required to decipher and understand the material. Sometimes it is hard enough for us to understand the nuances of *today's* writers. How much harder it is to catch all the implications of a record representing a society long gone.

From these considerations it should be clearly evident that the reader of any history book is greatly dependent on the knowledge and good judgment of the historian who evaluates the record.

Too Many Records. So far, we have noted that a historian, in attempting to reconstruct the past, is sometimes thwarted by lack of pertinent records or by the unreliability of available ones. But has it occurred to you that a historian is often embarrassed by the sheer volume, the towering mountains, of pertinent information at his disposal?

This is especially true in the case of more recent history. Pity the poor doctoral candidate writing a history of some phase of the Great Depression of the 1930s! Imagine the overwhelming volume of information calling for his attention—official federal, state and local government records; a flood of statistics; congressional and state hearings and debates; newspaper and magazine accounts; memoirs; records of business firms and labor unions; commentaries by economists, sociologists and political scientists; the testimony of numerous individuals eager to describe how bad things were. The number of sources appears endless. Or put yourself in the position of the group of historians preparing the official United States Army chronicle of World War 2, who faced the task of sifting through 17,120 tons of records.

What do conscientious scholars do when confronted by

such a Mount Everest of material? They do their best. They begin by sampling it in some organized and rational fashion. But they can rarely be sure that these samples reflect a typical cross section of the material as a whole, or that some highly significant facts have not been missed.

The Role of the Historian

In almost every case, the historian accumulates far more information about the subject than can be included in the volume he or she is writing. The resultant problem just cannot be avoided. The more important material must be separated from the less important, the former to be included, the latter to be left out. But how does one determine what is important and what is not? Obviously, there must be some standard of judgment. That standard can only be the historian's own system of values.

To complicate matters still further, most readers of historical works are not satisfied with a bare narrative of what happened in the past. They want some analysis and the author's conclusions about the significance of the events described.

In the nineteenth century there was a strong movement among historians to confine the writing of history to straight narrative. Its proponents claimed that history is a science in the same sense as chemistry or physics. It should be based on a strictly scientific, coldly clinical examination of the source material. Above all, the historian should not interpret the facts, but only describe them, leaving it up to the readers to draw their own conclusions. According to this movement, the historian should maintain strict neutrality on every issue of the past, not adhering to any ideological, political or religious point of view. The movement reflected the great admiration for scientific achievement that was so much a part of the nineteenth century.

This movement probably did some good in fighting undue bias and airy flights of fancy in describing the past. After all, narrating plainly and accurately what happened must be the historian's first priority. Nevertheless, this effort to make the historian's art a "science" was essentially a fizzle. It failed for a number of good reasons. In the first place, unlike the physical sciences, history deals largely with unique events. Then there is the crucial and inevitable role of the historian's personal value judgments and skill in selecting material to be included and excluded. As we shall develop at some length below, it is impossible for any historian to hold a completely neutral view of the past.

But this effort failed also because the reader usually desires that the historian exercise value judgments. Presumably, after years of study the writer knows far more about the subject than the reader does. The reader understandably wishes to know what conclusions the historian has reached after long years of study.

Some time ago while in graduate school, I prepared a bibliographical report on Oliver Cromwell, the immensely controversial leader of the Puritan Commonwealth in seventeenth-century England. I consulted thirty-eight different Cromwell biographies in my effort to discover what the experts thought about Cromwell's character, performance and legacy. I remember feeling cheated upon finding that the expert who knew most about Cromwell, who had spent a lifetime researching his character and career, gave no conclusion at all. Of course, I could make up my own mind on the basis of the information gathered, and eventually that would be my responsibility. But in the meantime I felt we students deserved to have some guidance from the scholar best able to make a value judgment.

Furthermore, bare facts about the past, without any comments concerning their significance—without any admiration or blame, without passion—tend to be lifeless and dull, sometimes even meaningless. We want the historian to display some warmth and feeling—within reason. The historian who could describe slavery or Nazi and Soviet concentration camps without a sense of outrage must have veins filled with antifreeze rather than blood. But all this poses problems for the reader, who wonders if the historian's emotional attachments have clouded his objectivity.

Obviously, most events recorded by historians are, for practical purposes, incontrovertible. It would serve no useful object, for example, to question that William of Normandy invaded England in 1066 or that Franklin D. Roosevelt was elected president of the United States in 1932. Enough "facts" are open to controversy, however, to justify caution.

But here readers are often at a disadvantage, particularly when studying a segment of history for the first time. (This is true in other academic disciplines as well.) Readers may not know when the author is taking sides on a controversial subject, since they are not aware that there *is* any controversy. Nor can they be cognizant of important facts that the author may have omitted. Unless they read very carefully, they may not notice when the author passes from statement of fact to expression of personal judgment. On debatable points the author is justified in expressing his opinion. But he should not present opinion, no matter how informed, as fact.

Identifying the Historian's Perspective

So here we have a crucial problem concerning our view of the past and thus our understanding of the world we live in. We do not have the past before us to view for ourselves. Except for the rare occasions when we can personally examine the original records, we have only the records as selected, evaluated and interpreted by the historian. These records are subject to the historian's predispositions, attitudes and biases. In short, the historical record is filtered through the mind of the historian before it reaches the reader or listener.

This is not said in criticism of historians, since the situation is unavoidable. Every individual, without exception, views the past, present and future from his or her own perspective. This perspective is the product of intrinsic personal traits, environment, education, affections, economic standing, national and political loyalties, religious background and many other factors, recognized and unrecognized, that distinguish the human being from the machine. Most historians are honest and conscientious. They describe the past as they see it. But what they see is colored by the tint of the glasses they wear.

A historian from a developing country such as Kenya, anticipating a future dominated by the so-called Third World, will naturally look at the world and its historical past from a perspective different from that of an Englishman whose memory is filled with the glories of an empire almost gone. Historians identified with the radical left will differ in their perspective from historians identified with the moderate middle or the radical right. My whole generation was profoundly influenced by our emergence into the adult world during the Great Depression. We tend to lack the assurance that often characterizes generations brought up in more affluent times. It will be obvious to every reader that this paragraph was written by a history professor looking at the past from a Western perspective. An Indian or Chinese professor, even if a Christian, would probably reflect a different perspective.

Of course, we must not carry this point too far. Among historians of all sorts of persuasions there is general agreement on many historical matters, especially on what constitutes the facts as opposed to the interpretation of those facts. The fact that Israel won the Six-Day War remains unchanged, whether it is recorded by an Israeli or an Arab. But what that victory proved is still debatable.

When reading any historical work it is a good idea to try to learn enough about the author to identify the perspective from which he or she views the past. Such information is sometimes not readily available, but a librarian will help you find whatever data is at hand. When studying the development of Marxism, for instance, it is useful to know whether or not the author is himself a Marxist. Or, when reading a book about the Reformation, it is helpful to know whether the author is a Roman Catholic, Protestant or non-Christian. This is not to imply that we cannot gain valuable insights from historians of perspectives different from our own. We certainly can. But knowing the orientation of the writer does alert us to the implications of his treatment of controversial questions. Some historians state explicitly what their frame of reference is. For instance, William L. Shirer, in the foreword to his immensely popular *The Rise and Fall of the Third Reich,* said flatly that he detested all totalitarian dictatorships in principle and loathed Hitler's in particular for what he had personally seen of that regime in action.[1] The student finds such advance notice very helpful.

History through Christian Glasses
Viewing history from one's own perspective is unavoidable. But this is not always recognized.

Christian historians and history instructors in particular have been harshly criticized for viewing history from a fixed, that is, a Christian, point of view. Critics claim that Christians, because of the primacy of their commitment to Christ and to biblical teachings, lack objectivity. They say, in fact, that Christians have prejudged the past by taking a predetermined position on historical questions. Christians supposedly do not see the past clearly because they are wearing highly colored religious spectacles.

Christian writers *have* at times been guilty of distortion. But the critics ignore the fact that they, themselves, wear glasses of some tint; that is, they hold very basic presuppositions which affect the way they "see" historical evidence. As mentioned before, everyone, without exception, views history from some observation point. In the case of these particular critics, is it possible that their criticism of the Christian historian betrays a decided *anti*-Christian perspective? A critic in a professional evaluation recently commented negatively on a Christian instructor's approach to history:

I firmly believe that the study of history must be approached from a purely secular ... point of view and that Christianity represents a set of ideological and intellectual attitudes which are a part of history and do not transcend it.[2]

This critic certainly has a right to his own approach to history, but he seems to have overlooked the fact that his "purely secular" approach is as much a personal perspective as that of the Christian historian whom he criticized. When he states that Christianity does not transcend history, he denies the supernatural nature of our faith—hardly a neutral position. Furthermore, he fails to recognize the faith that he holds himself: faith in his ability to find objective, historical facts; faith that history can be described in purely mechanistic terms; and faith that God will never intervene in history.

Occasionally you will encounter writers or teachers of history who do not even present a facade of neutrality, but are quite frank and explicit in their opposition to the Christian faith. Randy, a college student, tells in his own words about an experience he had.

We were studying slavery. The professor was showing slides of slaves in chains and nets that were so gross, you could hardly look at them. While he was showing them, "Amazing Grace" was playing over the public-address system. When the song ended, he launched into a bitter attack on Christianity. He stated that John Newton, the author of "Amazing Grace," was a hypocrite because he was a captain of slave ships.

I didn't know a thing about John Newton, but I felt that

anybody who could write a song like "Amazing Grace" had to have a genuine Christian walk. I spent that night reading about John Newton's life. I found out that he gave up slave trading after he became a Christian. It was after he gave it up that he wrote "Amazing Grace." In fact, he worked to abolish it. He influenced William Wilberforce, who was the man who led the successful fight to abolish slavery in the British Empire.

The next day I asked the professor for time to answer his unfair treatment of Christianity. He agreed in the name of academic freedom, and several of the students in the class were impressed by my findings.[3]

Christians view the past from a Christian perspective because they view *everything* that way if their faith is more than a superficial pose. Christians are to have the mind of Christ (Phil. 2:5) and to "take every thought captive to obey Christ" (2 Cor. 10:5). They are to walk so close to their Master and open their hearts so completely to the Holy Spirit, that their mental processes, values, affections and attitudes are those of Christ. They are to do everything "to the glory of God" (1 Cor. 10:31).

It follows then that the Christian's view of the human past will be unique. No one is truly a Christian who confines the authority of Christ to a narrowly religious fragment of life, while leaving crucial concerns—including the past of the human race—to secular jurisdiction.

Note that what we are discussing here is a Christlike *attitude* toward the past. We are not implying that every Christian necessarily has a highly developed Christian philosophy of history, always judges rightly or will interpret the past in exactly the same way as another Christian.

A biblical perspective on history should act as ballast for the Christian historian. The modern world, including the world of the historian, has been swept by wave after wave of intellectual enthusiasms. During the 1930s, for instance, a time of grave unemployment and other economic hardships, history was typically interpreted in terms of business "booms and busts" and how to avoid the "busts." During World War 2, the emphasis was on recurring struggles between liberty and tyranny. After the conflict, the "one world" concept was stressed, followed by the cold war. During the 1960s, there came a wave of iconoclasm, under which almost all institutions inherited from the past were tried and found wanting. In the 1970s, a reaction set in against deep ideological commitments.

Christian historians and students of history cannot be, and should not be, untouched by such currents. They must, after all, address themselves to the problems of their time. On the other hand, they need not be engulfed by those currents. The Christian faith provides a structure of basic truths which transcends the waves and gives a certain detachment needed to correctly evaluate the passing storm. In the words of the Apostle Paul: "Do not be conformed to this world but be transformed by the renewal of your mind, that you may prove what is the will of God, what is good and acceptable and perfect" (Rom. 12:2).

Some Perspectives on Historical Perspectives
A further qualification is necessary to avoid confusion concerning what I have said about historical perspectives. I have stated that everyone, without exception, looks at the past (indeed, at all of life) from his or her own perspective. Therefore, Christians are to be encouraged to view the past from a genuinely Christian perspective. This does not imply, however, tolerance either of those who fail to tell the whole pertinent truth or of those who unfairly present the facts. The opposite is true. Having the mind of Christ should provide every possible impulse toward the most sensitive truthfulness. It is the worst imaginable reflection on our Christian faith to imply that it needs falsehood or avoidance of rele-

vant facts to gain or to keep adherents.

When we write about any event from one particular perspective, we do not necessarily imply that another person looking at the same event from another vantage point is necessarily wrong. Mount Rainier looks quite different when viewed from Paradise Valley than when viewed from Sunrise. General Washington and Lord Cornwallis might submit two different reports on the Battle of Yorktown. Both might be accurate, but Cornwallis in the hour of defeat might be excused for writing about the event from a somewhat more pessimistic viewpoint.

But this does not suggest that every perspective is as valid as every other. Each must be appraised on its own merits. Each view of the drama of the past is only as clear as the lorgnette the playgoer uses. For example, the Nazis looked at history from a warped perspective because their whole ideology was warped. If Marxism is basically a valid system, Marxist versions of history will be basically valid. If Marxism is a flawed system, the history it produces will also be flawed. By the same token, the Christian perspective on the human past must be judged by the validity of Christianity itself. If the Christian faith is a tissue of myths, it can only provide a mythological view of the past. But if the Bible is true, and if Jesus Christ is really "the way, and the truth, and the life" as he claims, then the Christian's view of the past will be the clearest of all.

A problem arises, however, from the fact that no Christian, even when unreservedly committed to Christ, is only a Christian and nothing else. We are Christians *and* Americans or Canadians or Chileans or whatever. We are Christians *and* members of social and occupational groupings. We must continually be on our guard to distinguish between perspectives that are uniquely Christian and those that reflect these other aspects of our backgrounds.

Christianity and the Time Dimension 3

The ancients did not look at history in the same way we do today. They had little to say about the remote past, probably partly due to the absence of written records. Tales of long ago were handed down by word of mouth by poets, who were more interested in their story value than in a factual series of events bound together by cause and effect. There were annals (bare lists of occurrences) and tedious genealogies of kings and priests, but little effort to promote any understanding of the flow of events over long periods of time.

The Wheel of Time

Typically, the pagan ancients thought of history in terms of cycles. They conceived of time as a great wheel turning round and around. There had been a golden age of good laws and human happiness in the faraway past. The present was a period of degeneration, but when the wheel had again turned full circle the golden age would be temporarily restored. This would be followed, of course, by another period of decay. Time was the enemy of man. Nothing really new ever happened. The whole of history was rather meaningless. Some carried the idea to an extreme, claiming (if it were applied to today) that sometime in the future, in another turn of the wheel, there would be another John Jones or another Mary Smith exactly like you. Not even the human personality was really unique.

Under the circumstances, it is not surprising that the historians among even the intellectually sophisticated Greeks wrote principally of their own times or the very recent past. Herodotus, admired as the "Father of History," in writing about the climactic struggle between the Greeks and Persians, carried his narrative down to events occurring within his own lifetime. The equally famous Thucydides actually participated personally in the Peloponnesian War which he so honestly described.

It is also significant to note *why* these men wrote their histories. In the introduction to his work, Herodotus stated that he was anxious to

> preserve from decay the remembrance of what men have done, and [to prevent] the great and wonderful actions of the Greeks and the Barbarians from losing their due meed of glory; and withal to put on record what were the grounds of their feud.[1]

In Book I of his *History of the Peloponnesian War,* Thucydides expressed the hope that his work would

> be judged useful by those inquirers who desire an exact knowledge of the past as an aid to the interpretation of the future, which in the course of human things must resemble if it does not reflect it.[2]

Both confined themselves to limited subjects. Neither detailed the history of Greece over long reaches of time. Neither addressed himself to the meaning of history as a whole, if, in fact, he thought it had a meaning. The value of history lay in contemplation of the immediate event or movements of comparatively short duration.

Time Has Purpose and Meaning

In the light of such attitudes toward history, how very revolutionary was history as portrayed in the Bible. The *whole* of history has profound meaning because it is bound up with the purposes of God. It has direction and movement. It begins with a golden age in the Garden of Eden and records the fall of man through sin, but it does not go round and around in a wearisome cycle. Humans are not the playthings of inexorable fate, but creations of a living God with whom they can interact. The Old Testament pictures history moving forward to a glorious goal crowned by the coming of the Messiah-Redeemer. The New Testament describes his coming and predicts his coming again to establish a kingdom which will have no end. Here we have not a wheel moving slowly around to where it began, but a purposive story with a beginning and an ending.

Today some, but emphatically not all, key aspects of this revolutionary view of history are taken for granted by most people in the Western world—even those who deny the authority of the Bible. The majority of those who think seriously about history think in terms of a beginning and a linear movement through the centuries to the present and on into the future. They attach some meaning to the entire flow of time. Even while denying the basis of the Christian's hope, some have thought that this flow entailed progress toward some utopia of the future. (See pp. 60-67.) Others have simply adopted a linear view of history and have discarded the Hebrew notion of progress toward a goal.

The Hebrews were the only people of the ancient world who had a sense of the whole course of history. It began with Creation, Eden and the Fall and, therefore, embraced all humanity. They were supremely conscious of themselves as God's chosen people, a role that involved not only a relationship but a historical event—God's choice of their father Abraham at a certain place and time in history. They had a compelling, gripping history which inspired both pride and contrition—deliverance from bondage in Egypt, cowardice in the desert, conquest of the Promised Land, the glorious imperial days of David and Solomon, repeated defeats due to ingratitude and infidelity, repeated comebacks under inspiring leaders, eventual exile and dispersion, the enduring promise of a new kingdom under a new David through whom all the nations of the earth would be blessed. It was a history that demanded remembering and retelling. Each incident had its own meaning and lesson, but all the incidents were tied together by cause and effect and by the purposes of God.

Did you ever stop to think that God actually *commanded* the study of history? He instituted for the Hebrews the feast of the Passover, a re-enactment of that pivotal historical event when Pharaoh "let God's people go," and the Hebrews began their career as a politically independent community. In future generations when children asked what the observance meant. Parents were to be prepared to answer with a wonderful chapter from their people's history (Ex. 12:24-27). Again, when the Hebrews crossed the Jordan to Canaan, they were commanded to erect a monument of twelve stones to commemorate the event. Then when their children asked, "What do these stones mean to you?" (Josh. 4:6) they would have a good opportunity to relate another chapter describing God's work in their country's past.

Time and time again they were admonished to remember the days of old as inspiration and warning and to cement their awareness of themselves as a distinct people. For them, religion and history were intertwined at almost every point. Of special import to us here is the fact that Christians from the very beginning embraced these historical events as integral parts of their own faith. Christianity is incomprehensible without this Hebrew, Old Testament background and its view of history.

A Historical Religion?

When Christians assert that Christianity is a historical religion, we are not merely saying that it is a very old religion or even that it is linked to stirring historical events. Every religion is a historical religion in the sense that it had a birth and a founder and development over a period of time. Nor do we mean merely that Christian truth is revealed through history. We claim much more than that. We are saying that although some aspects of our faith (such as the purposes of God in creation) are beyond time and historical investigation, certain concrete historical events are the very fabric of our faith. God became a human being and was born into the world at a certain historical place and time. He was crucified on a very tangible cross at a specified place, Jerusalem, during the reign of a specific Roman emperor, Tiberius. And then there was the resurrection! The validity of the Christian faith and the Christian's hope of eternal life ride on whether these alleged historical events did, or did not, actually happen.

Even while denying his divinity, few deny that Jesus was born or even that he died on the cross. But did he rise from the dead and was he seen by about five hundred persons in the ensuing forty days? Did he ascend into heaven? These are flat-out historical questions, subject to historical verification. If these events did not occur, we have a beautiful story but a futile hope. St. Paul put it bluntly: "If Christ has not been raised, then our preaching is in vain and your faith is in vain" (1 Cor. 15:14). Small wonder that the first Christians made such a commotion testifying to the resurrection and celebrating Christ's victory over death. They made the commemoration of that victory their first great festival.

What a sharp contrast we see, then, between Christianity, firmly rooted in concrete historical events, and its early rivals, built around symbolic myths. The gods and goddesses (of love, war, harvest, wind or whatever) of Christianity's first rivals quarreled, made love, celebrated or suffered—but only in fertile human imaginations. How many of their devotees believed that these goings on ever really happened in a concrete historical sense?

During the first two centuries, Christ's chief rival was Mithras, hero of a pagan cult originating in Persia. Mithraism had some attractive features. It emphasized courage and virtue, Mithras being the champion of goodness and light in the struggle against darkness and evil. But in many respects it was quite typical of the alternatives to Christianity. According to the cult, Mithras was "born out of a rock at the dawn of day" and eventually rode to heaven in the chariot of the sun. An appealing story, but such events were symbolic rather than real. What was the geographic location of that rock and the date of that ascension? Contrast with this the down-to-earth realism of the gospel, firmly anchored in history with dates and places.

From your study of the New Testament you may have learned that one of the most dangerous threats to the early church was the heresy which claimed that the facts of the gospel were mere symbols of hidden truth. This heresy impelled the Apostle John, a most intimate witness to Christ's life on earth, to remind his converts that his message concerning Christ involved that "which we have seen with our eyes, which we have looked upon and touched with our hands" (1 Jn. 1:1). Even today we still hear echoes of the first-century pseudo-Christianity that John was fighting.

Since the very basis of the Christian faith hinges on the validity of historical events, how can we ever be contemptuous of history?

The Christian faith is subject to historical scrutiny in another way: What has been the effect of Christianity on world history over the past two thousand years? This is far too broad a question to be answered in a brief treatment such as this, but Christians cannot avoid the issue. The books written on the subject, by both defenders and critics of Christianity, would fill your history classroom. Unfortunately, the discussion typically has been too narrow—involving only the activities of conspicuous leaders. Or it has gone rather far afield, centering on the church as a human institution (for example, a department of the state), focusing on struggles in which the name *Christian* was a cover for purely secular aims or describing activities of people professing to be Christian but displaying no real commitment to Christ or his teaching.

Obviously, a discussion of the effect of Christianity on world history should include such indirect or blurred factors. But a more pertinent treatment of the question must center around the conduct and influence of a host of humbler but often more genuine Christians down through the centuries. What has been the influence of thousands of unsung, but dedicated priests and ministers faithfully teaching a gospel of love, redemption and hope from pulpits not only in the centers of power but in obscure parishes where people live and work? What has been the impact of unpretentious laypeople in towns and villages who have believed and practiced the Christian message? How have earnest Christian parents down through the years influenced the future in the rearing of their children? Questions such as these are immeasurably more difficult to answer than those involving the doings of popes and prelates or the proceedings of great church conclaves. But they focus more directly on the essential issue.

We should be greatly encouraged by the fact that our Christian faith has survived for nearly two thousand years the attacks of its foes, the neglect of the indifferent and especially the clammy embrace of false friends. It has met the needs of high and low, rich and poor, young and old, simple and sophisticated on every continent. It has been analyzed, dissected, compared, interpreted, mythicized and demythologized, snarled and simplified. And still millions in all walks of life accept it as their rule of life and their hope for eternity.

In the last analysis, however, the Christian gospel must be judged not by the magnitude of its impact on world history or even its survival value, but on whether or not it brings eternal life to those who trust in Christ. History enthusiasts must be careful to keep things in proper proportion.

History and "Redemption History"

In the preceding chapter we pointed out that there are two contrasting ways of looking at history from the Christian viewpoint—a great drama of Fall and redemption, and the more limited narratives of human events. We emphasized that "redemption history" finds the meaning of the whole course of human history in a source outside that history and thus lies beyond the province of ordinary historical proof as provided by documentary material. "Classroom history," on the other hand, deals with more "mundane" human events potentially verifiable by the kind of evidence we have discussed.

With which of these two kinds of history are the Bible and the Christian faith concerned? Obviously, with both. At the very heart of the Christian view of the past are: God's work of creation; the idyllic joys of Eden; the Fall of mankind through sin; redemption through the Incarnation, death and resurrection of Christ; and the anticipation of a coming reign of righteousness beyond history.

At the same time, the Bible illustrates that individual, concrete human events are immensely instructive and important. The Scriptures describe such events by the hundreds—the call of Abraham, Pharaoh's daughter finding the baby Moses, the military exploits of David, the confrontations between King Ahab and Elijah, the career of Daniel in the courts of Babylon, Queen Esther and the plots of Haman, Jesus' dealings with Pharisees and publicans, the wedding at Cana, the walk to Emmaus, Peter's sermon on the day of Pentecost, Paul's encounter with the silversmiths of Ephesus. The list goes on and on in great variety, involving prophets and priests, kings and queens, soldiers and statesmen, nobles and shepherds, city folk and farmers, Jews and Greeks, men, women and children, the good, the bad, the indifferent. The Bible certainly teaches that individuals and what they do *are* important. This is a warning against becoming so exclusively involved in "God's great plan for the ages" that we banish human beings from the pages of history.

If actions of human beings great and small were important and significant in biblical times, is it not reasonable to believe they have continued to be important in the centuries since? If the Bible includes so many human events for their instructional value, should that not encourage us to study other areas of history also for the lessons they teach?

At the opposite extreme, many history instructors are so thoroughly immersed in researching and teaching about specific human events that they display hostility toward any attempt to discern some transcendental purpose or meaning to the totality of human history. I remember the subject coming up in a university seminar and the professor calling any such attempt "sublime nonsense."

Several factors seem to contribute to this hostility. First, some historians, true to their own materialist or humanist convictions, are wary of any claims to knowledge derived through supernatural revelation and involving themes beyond the limits of human experience.

Second, historians have invested their professional lives

in the laborious gathering and meticulous study of source documents and the findings of other scholars—labors which they consider the true role of the historian. Consequently, they have little patience with any claim to knowledge which short-circuits this toilsome process. This impatience has at times been a reaction to works of shabby scholarship (in which conjecture poses as fact) that have sneaked onto the shelves of Christian bookstores everywhere.

Third, professional historians often feel that questions of ultimate meaning lie outside the historian's field of expertise. The most highly competent professional historian in the world has no special claim to insights in such matters. "Let's confine ourselves to the knowable," some seem to say. "Don't bother us with the unknowable." Others, while recognizing the validity of such heavy questions, feel they are more properly left to the religion or philosophy departments. This latter group includes some thoughtful and knowledgeable Christian historians who feel they must and can keep their professional and devotional lives separate. Do you believe this is possible?

Looking Both Ways

Up to a point we can sympathize with such sentiments. Scholars who ponder God's eternal plan for the ages and scholars who study peasant life in medieval France or the colonial policies of Kaiser Wilhelm II live in different academic worlds. It is not easy to cross from one to the other. On the other hand, from the standpoint of the Christian student trying to make sense out of the past, such hostility is confusing and raises several important questions.

In the first place, can we separate our thinking into two compartments without succumbing to academic schizophrenia? Can we divorce our study of concrete historical events, verifiable through surviving records, from our contemplation of the meaning of history as a whole? This type of problem has agitated profound thinkers for centuries.

Second, doesn't just about everybody who has thought about the subject at all, have *some* ideas, formulated or unformulated, about the meaning of humanity's total experience here on earth? And can these ideas fail to influence a person's attitude toward specific events?

It would obviously be awkward and undesirable for historians to try to relate everything they write about to ultimate reality. Sooner or later, however, should they not come to grips with the question of ultimate meaning? Is it not the historians' proud boast that they can illuminate the underlying meaning of the past? Should they be satisfied with explaining the parts but avoid their relation to the whole? Is there any reason why historians should not go to the philosopher and the theologian for help? After all, they constantly consult with political scientists, economists, sociologists, anthropologists, geographers, psychologists and a host of other experts for help in understanding various phases of the past.

These issues are of momentous significance to the Christian. In a sense, the two kinds of history we have discussed meet in the person of Jesus Christ—eternal Son of God and first-century carpenter of Nazareth. Our Christian faith encompasses events beyond time and space of which only the faint shadow can be discerned by the human eye. But it also maintains that God himself became a human being on this planet and involved himself in tangible, material human events recorded by eyewitnesses and subject to documentary examination. We believe that God can use both revelation and scholarly research to enlighten us concerning the past and that every area of knowledge can be illuminated by the Holy Spirit.

But to avoid confusion, it is important to note which kinds of knowledge are and are not susceptible to the methods of critical historical investigation. We must bear in mind the limits of the two kinds of history. Knowledge, through divine revelation, of God's great plan of redemption may not necessarily give us any special insights into changes in Soviet farming techniques or the military strategies of the Spanish conquistadors. Lessons in these matters must be learned through the patient study of pertinent historical records. On the other hand, our knowledge of such "mundane subjects" does not *in itself* necessarily give us any special insights into God's eternal purposes.

A danger here is the temptation to dismiss such "mundane subjects" as irrelevant to a Christian view of the past. To do so would be a serious mistake. Christians know that God is at work in every area of their individual lives, not merely in that which might be labeled *spiritual*. It follows then that God in the same manner is at work in so-called mundane history. The problem is to discover how we can know in what way God is working, since the ordinary tools of historical scholarship do not lend themselves to this kind of investigation.

Patterns in the Past

4

In this chapter we scrutinize more closely some suggested answers to one of the most basic questions raised by a study of history: Is there an overall pattern to the past?

If we put all the known facts of history together, do they form a discernible, meaningful design? Is there a golden key that unlocks the underlying meaning of human experience here on earth? Is there some profound kernel of truth around which we can arrange the events of history in meaningful formation?

These are heavy questions, to be sure. When we ponder them we join the ranks of thoughtful men and women who for centuries have been challenged by the central enigma of the human experience. Certainly such questions deserve our careful attention.

Obviously, in a brief introduction we cannot discuss in detail even the best known among the scores of theories concerning the essential meaning of human history. All we can do here is capsulize a few samples, always keeping in mind how they relate to our Christian faith.

Chuck the Whole Question

One group has given up trying to find any meaning in historical events. Some point out that we really do not know enough about the past to make it worthwhile to bother with such questions. How can we discern a pattern in the tapestry of time when we have only scattered bits of the fabric available to scrutinize, when hundreds of millions of people have lived and died without leaving any evidence that they existed? We find it difficult enough to understand even the bits and pieces of history that we do have.

Others take the opposite tack but come up with the same conclusion. They say that despite the great gaps in our knowledge of the past, the sum total of what has been uncovered is so colossal that no single human mind can come close to comprehending it all. The portion that one person can grasp is such a small part of this enormous canvas of knowledge that it would be presumptuous for anyone to draw any conclusions about the whole. This would be like trying to describe the geology, flora and fauna of the whole Rocky Mountain range on the basis of what can be observed on an afternoon stroll. We ought to recognize our limitations.

Adding to this dilemma is the present state of the profession. More and more scholars are entering the field. Meticulous research is bringing to light more and more information about every corner of the past. The printing presses grind out more and more monographs on every conceivable historical subject. Old conclusions are discarded on the basis of new evidence. Even specialists in narrow historical fields complain that, try as they might, they cannot keep up with the new publications even in their own speciality. If specialists are reluctant to generalize about their own narrow fields, how can we make profound generalizations about the entire sweep of history?

This reluctance to look for patterns is not an all-or-nothing stance. Many historians are willing to search for and describe a meaningful pattern in a portion of history which they consider manageable—the history of the United States, for instance, or even some longer period such as the Middle Ages. But this is not quite the same thing as trying to explain the basic meaning of the whole human experience here on earth.

The alleged impossibility of mastering the whole field of history to the point where one can discern an overall, meaningful pattern is well illustrated by criticisms leveled at the renowned British historian, Arnold Toynbee (1889-1975), whose *A Study of History* in twelve volumes encompasses twenty-one developed civilizations and several "arrested" ones.[1]

Through his wide-ranging knowledge and his appealing literary style enriched by classical allusions and dramatic metaphors, Toynbee attracted an unusually large reading audience for so serious a work and thus stimulated interest in the big questions of history. Professional historians, however, are less than enthusiastic.

Critics claim that in tackling the whole range of human history Toynbee embarked on an impossible project for a single historian. When writing about his own specialty— ancient Greece and to some extent the Islamic world—he was on strong ground. But specialists in other fields of history claim that his knowledge of their areas was quite inadequate. Thus we ask, If so erudite a scholar as Toynbee could not comprehend the whole of history, is the full sweep of the past too vast a subject for the human mind to grasp? Some scholars seem to answer, Yes. With regard to the question of whether or not there is a pattern to past events, they feel that the answer is beyond our reach.

History Is Chaos

Others accept these questions about the meaning of the totality of history as legitimate and pertinent and then proceed to answer them with a simple, No. There is no meaningful pattern to the entire expanse of history. They emphasize that each individual is a separate fountain of action. Human nature is fickle, people's decisions unpredictable. Thus the events of history flit from wisdom to folly, from vice to virtue, with no system or consistency. History is chaos. It is nowhere near as coherent and rational as many historians picture it.

These "chaos" historians go on to claim that those who do ascribe a pattern to the past do so by ignoring the facts that do not fit the pattern and forcing the rest into a preconceived groove. They insist that it is an essential fact of the human condition that each individual person is a spiritual entity in his or her own right with the awesome responsibility to make personal decisions. Therefore, we badly misread the past when we ignore that human responsibility and claim that human beings are caught in the web of some historical necessity to which all decisions must conform.

An Existentialist Approach. As you can guess, such lines of thought fit easily into an existentialist philosophy of life. Since no meaning can be found in history as a whole or in long reaches of time, the thing to do is to concentrate on each moment's experience or wring from each individual historical event all the meaning it can yield. They say the historian should not coldly and methodically dissect a historical episode as though it were a frog in a biology lab. The way to understand and learn the lessons of the past is to wear the shoes of the real, warm-blooded human beings who participated in an event and try to learn how they felt and what inner motives impelled them to act as they did.

These historians maintain, either explicitly or implicitly, that such efforts can be significant and absorbing to the point where we do not need patterns or broad aerial views of history. Or they claim that the lack of positive answers about the human experience is part of the human predicament and we must face such uncertainties with whatever equanimity and poise we can muster.

A variation on this theme professed by some Christian scholars maintains that there may be order and meaning to history but this inner meaning will remain hidden from human eyes until it is revealed by God. Since the meaning is not revealed by the events themselves, we should give up trying to make sense out of history and just take the "leap of faith" that God will reveal the meaning in his own good time.

Chaos and the Christian. How should you and I as Christians respond to the history-as-chaos perspective? Does it or does it not harmonize with our Christian faith?

Clearly this school of thought raises some interesting questions. Is it not at least sometimes true that those who diagram the past according to a simple blueprint usually omit a multitude of inconvenient facts that do not fit and force the facts they do use into the pattern they believe they have discerned? Is there not a tendency to leave the dilemmas and ambiguities of flesh-and-blood individuals out of the study of human history?

Does not the Bible teach that each human being is a spiritual entity responsible for his or her own decisions? Is not a substantial part of the Scriptures devoted to narratives concerning the lives and dilemmas of individuals involved in immediate, concrete situations, as contrasted to long-range movements or abstract principles? And does not the Bible make it clear that human conduct is fickle and unpredictable? Even Bible greats such as Abraham, Jacob, David, Elijah and Peter acted quite inconsistently—sometimes virtuously and wisely, sometimes perversely.

On the other hand, is the Bible merely a collection of unconnected narratives of individual events without a central theme or transcending purpose? Does not the theme of redemption of a fallen and sinful humanity run like a scarlet thread from Genesis to Revelation? Do we as Christians have convictions about God and his dealings with humanity that make it difficult for us to accept the idea that history has no unifying theme?

Perhaps we do not have to accept or reject the whole chaotic theory intact. The fact that we cannot comprehend the entire meaning of the entire past does not mean that we cannot understand some of it or that we should give up trying to understand more.

Whether or not we accept the conclusions of this school of historians, it does teach us two useful lessons. It warns us against unwarranted pride in the face of a subject so vast in its implications as to defy comprehension. And it jolts us back to the realization that history deals primarily with real human beings, not cold abstractions. Conversely, it is only one short step from the idea that history is just one big, meaningless mess to the conclusion that our individual lives are meaningless too. Christians know better than that.

The Music Goes Round and Around

The history of the past is a mere puppet show.—A little man comes out and blows a little trumpet, and goes in again.—You look for something new, and lo! another little man comes out and blows another little trumpet, and goes in again.—And it is all over.[2]

"Cyclists" in the Ancient World. We began chapter three with a brief discussion of the ancients' concept of history as an endless series of cycles. In pagan antiquity there was little or no thought of history in terms of process or development. To Aristotle, the great encyclopedic mind of fourth-century B.C. Greece, the "polis" or community was timeless. The Greeks taught that in the distant past there had been a golden

age of good laws and human happiness. The present was a period of degeneration, but some bright future day new law-givers would appear to restore the golden age of the past. Unfortunately, this glorious age would not last but would degenerate into another period of decay and unhappiness. And so the wheel of time went round and around. You will note here a strong suggestion that blind fate is in control and the very best a man or woman can do is endure the smiles and frowns of fortune with courage and fortitude.

In this connection, there has been considerable misapprehension about the first chapter of Ecclesiastes in the Bible.

The sun rises and the sun goes down,
    and hastens to the place where it rises.
The wind blows to the south,
    and goes round to the north;
round and round goes the wind,
    and on its circuits the wind returns.
All streams run to the sea,
    but the sea is not full;
to the place where the streams flow,
    there they flow again.
What has been is what will be,
    and what has been done is what will be done;
    and there is nothing new under the sun.
Is there a thing of which it is said,
    "See, this is new"?
It has been already, in the ages before us.
(Eccles. 1:5-7, 9-10)

Some have erroneously concluded from this chapter that the Bible also teaches the cyclical theory of history. Nothing can be further from the truth. The writer of Ecclesiastes does not present this outlook as his own; he is describing the position of the materialists of his day, which he explodes at the end of the book.

The ancients' basically pessimistic and wearisome attitude toward history melts under the warm sun of the biblical message. The Hebrews alone among the ancient Near Eastern peoples thought of history not as a menacing thing but as a movement toward a glorious goal. Christians inherited this concept. They see in the Incarnation of God in Christ the focal point of all history, and look forward to his return— the event toward which all human history has been moving since the Fall.

Twentieth-century "Cyclists." The cyclical theory of history did not die with the ancients. Perhaps its longevity has been due in part to its affinity with the cycle of the seasons of the year. It is not difficult to understand how agrarian peoples, living close to the soil, would apply the cycle of planting, growth and harvest (or spring, summer, autumn and winter) to the history of their community, especially if they themselves saw little change from year to year.

In our own day, the cyclical theory is usually associated with the names of Oswald Spengler (1880-1936) and Arnold Toynbee. Of the two, Spengler was the more rigorous in his application of the theory. In his *Decline of the West* he claimed that civilizations are living organisms which undergo the same life cycle we do—birth, youth, maturity, senescence and death. Western civilization has already enjoyed the mature, creative stage and has entered the stage of reflection and material comfort. Spengler saw only decline and death in its future because it is impossible to reverse the life cycle.

Although many modern scholars share Spengler's pessimism, he has few strict followers today. It is difficult to believe that civilizations are organisms like the human body with the same life cycle of birth to an inevitable death.

Toynbee was a remarkably learned man and probably the most widely known historian of his day. In his *A Study of History* he examined twenty-one "developed" civilizations with the purpose of discovering, through the comparative method, laws of growth and decay. He concluded that civilizations are born in response to environmental challenges neither so severe as to thwart progress nor so favorable as to discourage creativity. Growth continues under the leadership of a creative elitist minority. But eventually the civilization breaks down, largely because the ruling minority becomes merely dominant and now lacks the creativity to meet new challenges.

These cycles of growth and decay remind us of the theory of the ancients. Toynbee differed from them, however, in his belief in a forward motion in history. The wheel goes around but the wagon moves forward, to use his own figure of speech.

Although Toynbee believed that (through the comparative method) he had found certain historical laws which not only explain the past but can help us predict probable future developments, he was far less deterministic than Spengler or the cyclical school in general. For instance, he did not believe Western civilization *has* to die. It can be rejuvenated through a religious (*religious*, not Christian) revival and consequent rebirth of the creative impulse.

In addition to their claim that Toynbee tackled a subject far too immense for a single human mind to comprehend, critics assert that Toynbee was more of a seer or prophet than a historian, bending the facts to fit his highly personalized, mystic vision of the rise and fall of civilizations. Christians may agree with his emphasis on the major role of religion in history, but they will differ sharply with his humanistic vision of the future—a single, peaceful, worldwide civilization under a world government and blessed by a religion representing "the best qualities of all religion." Does this dream not violate all that the Bible and human experience teach us about human nature without Christ?[3]

How valid is the cyclical concept? History as narrated in the Bible refutes the idea that human events reflect only a meaningless turning of the wheel of time. This refutation is confirmed by human experience. Recent times in particular bear little resemblance to any previous age. As we view today's population explosion, instant communication, space travel, nuclear weapons, widespread pollution and depletion of our natural resources, it is impossible to think of our day as representing just another turning of the wheel.

But in more limited spheres can we see the cyclical theory at work? In the scriptural history of the Hebrew people we see it quite clearly. The reign of a righteous king and worship of the one true God bring peace and prosperity. This period is followed by a time of idol worship, military defeat and misery during the reign of an unrighteous king. These tragic times in turn are followed by a revival under a new godly ruler. The cycle is repeated over and over again.

We can also see cycles in all kinds of human endeavors, including Christian movements. These movements are born in a great burst of enthusiasm to change the world, attracting people wholly committed to the cause. Such devoted effort brings rapid growth. Growth necessitates greater attention to organization, while success attracts new adherents lacking the self-sacrificing zeal of the founders. Eventually the movement is institutionalized and takes its comfortable place alongside others in respectable society, and the stage is set for a new movement, born in a great burst of enthusiasm, to change the world.

But all this does not suggest historical necessity. History does record occasional movements that experience a new baptism of fire. The cyclic chain of cause and effect *has* been broken. Maybe there is another lesson for us here.

The Role of the Hero
Most of us ordinary mortals make the best of situations as we find them. If our intelligence is equal to the situation, if we exercise conscientious effort—and maybe enjoy a bit of good

fortune—we achieve the measure of success that the opportunity offers.

But do you know a gifted individual who possesses not only these qualities but also the vision, imagination, drive and resourcefulness (and in some cases lack of scruple) to make his or her own opportunities? Do you know someone who decides what he wants to accomplish and then crashes through or circumvents all obstacles to achieve these aims?

If you do, you enjoy an advantage in understanding what we mean by the "great man" or "hero" (or great woman or heroine) theory of history.

As you probably surmise, the champions of this theory believe that the course of history has not been determined by impersonal forces, nor by mass humanity, but by the influence, decisions and actions of masterful individuals known to the trade as "heroes." Naturally, biographies of conspicuous individuals play an important part in this kind of history. In fact, some of its proponents go so far as to claim that "*all* history is biography."

This theory is most closely associated with Thomas Carlyle, nineteenth-century Scottish historian and essayist, who states:

> In all epochs of the world's history, we shall find the Great
> Man to have been the indispensable saviour of his epoch;
> —the lightning, without which the fuel never would have
> burnt. The History of the world, I said already, was the
> Biography of Great Men.[4]

Carlyle's book, *On Heroes, Hero-Worship, and the Heroic in History,* is the classic on the subject. Unfortunately, Carlyle was an opinionated dogmatist who introduced so many extraneous personal ideas into his treatment of the subject that his works do not serve as a very effective focus of discussion of the theory.[5]

Perhaps the best way to summarize the theory is to define just what we mean and do not mean by the words *great man* or *hero* in this context. By these labels we do not necessarily mean a morally worthy individual. We only mean that he or she has exercised decisive influence for either good or ill. Also, by *hero* we do not mean merely a famous person. Many famous people, entertainers, for instance, do little to affect the flow of history. Even rulers, army commanders and captains of industry may not qualify. We can easily recall several American presidents or European prime ministers who left little mark on the future. On the other hand, individuals who were relatively obscure in their lifetimes have sometimes exerted incalculable influence on future events. Such names as St. Paul and Karl Marx come readily to mind. The term includes heroes of thought as well as of action—anyone who, by his or her will and achievement, changed the course of history. We must distinguish between the "eventful" individual and the "event-making" individual. The former, by happening to be at the right place at the right time in the right position, makes the momentous decision; the latter not only makes the momentous decision but through extraordinary qualities of mind, personality and will sets up the situation that makes the decision possible.

Do Heroes Really Make the Difference? Bearing in mind the nature of the theory so described, we face the key question: To what extent has the current of history been guided by the hands of such masterful individuals?

Our thoughts in reply naturally turn to famous men and women in history who seem to have directed the flow of events—Alexander, Caesar, Charlemagne, Genghis Khan, Luther, Elizabeth of England, Cromwell, Peter the Great, Catherine the Great, Washington, Napoleon, Lenin, Hitler, Mao Tse-tung and a host of others.

Immediately questions arise to plague us. Would these individuals have been so dominant if the time had not been ripe for their particular brand of leadership? Could Napoleon have conquered most of Western Europe without the fiery nationalism and military organization inherited from the French Revolution? Could Hitler have grasped power in Germany without the special conditions produced by World War 1 and the Great Depression? How many prospective heroes have gone to their graves without having any opportunity to exercise their heroic talents? It raises the old question: Does the man make the event or the event make the man? Or does it work both ways?

Did all these people really change the course of history? Would the world be significantly different today if Lenin or Mao had fallen off a cliff in childhood? You may have heard the apocryphal story that American history was changed by a penknife: George Washington's mother supposedly offered him a penknife during his teens if he would forego joining the British Navy. Without his leadership could the thirteen bickering colonies have held together during the Revolution?

Did some of these famous heroes divine the direction events were already moving, and put themselves at the head of the column, perhaps making it move a bit faster? Do we overemphasize the role of conspicuous individuals and underestimate the role of their behind-the-scenes associates, or the role of molders of thought and opinion, or that of humbler men and women who have influenced the course of history in subtler ways?

Finally, to what extent can any individual, or even a group of individuals, change the course of history in the face of economic factors, the environment and other forces? Are the historians right who claim that the limits within which any individual can accomplish change are very, very narrow?

There are more questions here than answers. But that is as it should be. Try to think the questions through for yourself, rather than accepting at face value answers thrust upon you by someone else.

Here are a few more questions, this time about the implications of the hero theory. On the favorable side, does it suggest that we need not be the helpless victims of impersonal forces, but that we can, through intelligent leadership, attack our difficulties? Does it encourage us to recognize outstanding qualities of mind, will and spirit and thoughtfully and loyally to support competent leaders rather than succumbing to mediocrity?

On the other hand, by stressing the role of the strong and successful, does the theory lend itself to snobbery? If carried to an extreme might it not lead to authoritarianism, worship of success and power for their own sake and condonation of unscrupulous behavior as long as it leads to success? It might even lead to idol-worship, giving to men or women the veneration belonging only to God.

What does the Christian faith teach on the subject of heroes? The Bible places great emphasis on the decisive role of outstanding individuals. Did you ever wonder what would have happened if Abraham had refused to leave Ur of the Chaldees? if Moses had declined to lead Israel out of Egypt? if Joshua had turned back from the conquest of Canaan? if Paul had been disobedient to the heavenly vision? The disasters and eventual destruction that overtook the northern kingdom of Israel were due in large part to ungodly or weak leaders, while the repeated rallies and eventual survival of the Jewish people depended partly on inspired and godly leadership.

While God is not frustrated when the designated hero refuses to fulfill that role (as illustrated by the careers of Barak and Samson in the book of Judges), on the whole the Scriptures confirm again and again the crucial role of inspired leaders. But such human leadership is only one factor among many emphasized in the Bible narrative.

The Cult of Progress
When your great-grandfather was your age just about every-

body believed that the key to the whole sweep of history was "progress." The belief that humanity was climbing ever upward toward a golden age of unprecedented goodness, happiness and achievement was so pervasive in the Western world that the historian who did not share the general optimism was considered something of an oddity.

The experts were not thoroughly agreed about what progress meant, but the general feeling was that year by year, century by century, mankind was moving toward the day when material well-being would replace poverty and deprivation; rationality would replace myth and superstition; liberty and democracy would replace despotism and tyranny; a worldwide human brotherhood would replace hatred and war; and humanity would be the ruler rather than the victim of the forces of nature. Note the implication that while the conditions of life are constantly improving in quality, the human race itself is growing in both virtue and wisdom.

We need to go into some detail about this "cult of progress" because it illustrates a number of themes that are central to our discussion. We want to note the basis of the dream, why it flourished in the late eighteenth century and especially in the nineteenth century, and its main implications for the Christian student of history.

The New Jerusalem: Here or There?   We have emphasized that the world of pagan antiquity thought of history as a succession of cycles. The future held no real hope because recurring golden ages would always be followed by periods of decline and decadence. God's revelation to the Hebrews, on the other hand, involved a linear view of history, which eventually took the form of a forward look toward a glorious kingdom of righteousness, peace and prosperity under a new King David. Most of them understood this promise to be for the Jews only. Still, it was a radical departure from the weary hopelessness of the cyclical theory.

Christians, of course, were and are the heirs of the Old Testament revelation with its profound hope for the future. But Christ made clear that the future kingdom was offered not to the Jews only but to all people. And the new Jerusalem —the eternal kingdom of righteousness, love and joy— would not be an earthly kingdom climaxing human progress within history, but would be a heavenly kingdom that God himself would establish after he had decreed that time was at an end.

So we are left with the question, How was this expectation of a heavenly city beyond history transformed into the idea of progress within history—humanity progressing step by step toward a manmade golden age on this planet? The answer lies in the whole fabric of modern Western history. It is a subject that should attract your interest as you study the trend of Western thought during the past two or three hundred years. We can only summarize the main points here.

By the eighteenth century the pacesetters of Western thought had become more and more secular in their outlook. Human reason to a large extent had replaced divine revelation as the source of fundamental beliefs. But the decline of Christian faith naturally involved loss of the Christian hope of an age of happiness beyond time. The humanist scholars, habituated as they were by the Western, Christian tradition to look forward to a glorious future consummation of human history, offered in the place of the Christian hope a "Great Tomorrow" built by human reason and effort. That is why historians have called the cult of progress the "bastard offspring" of Christian doctrine and man-centered optimism.

The Century of Hope. It is not hard to understand why the idea of progress became so pervasive and immensely popular in the West in the nineteenth century. In that century science and technology produced all sorts of inventions that expanded the production of goods designed for human comfort and enjoyment; made a good start in the conquest of disease; triumphed over distance through the steamship, railroad and eventually the automobile; and gave every indication of producing more and more marvels in the future. Education flourished. Freedom and democracy seemed the wave of the future as popular government replaced old despotisms in a number of countries. Europe did not suffer a continent-wide war from 1815 to 1914. "Enlightened" European institutions reached primitive peoples around the world.

The epitome of the new optimistic spirit was the first world's fair, held in London in 1851, whose huge Crystal Palace attracted thirteen thousand exhibitors and six million visitors and gave dramatic visual demonstrations of human ingenuity and prowess. Without question it left the clear impression that human progress was indeed the key to all history.

The scholar who best represents the nineteenth-century reverence for science was undoubtedly Auguste Comte, "the father of sociology." He taught that there have been three stages of culture—the theological, the metaphysical and the positive (or scientific). These roughly represent, in ascending order, the dominance of religion, abstract reason or philosophy, and science.[6]

Also contributing to the nineteenth-century faith in irreversible progress was Darwinism, which taught that man is climbing ever upward from the brute, becoming more and more "human" in the process. The Darwinists tended to divide into two groups, both emphasizing human progress. One stressed progress through tough competition and the elimination of the ill-adapted (survival of the fittest). The other claimed that through evolution the human race had become so humane and competent that it was now capable of planning its own future and achieving progress through humanitarian reforms.

Marxism was also part of the cult. According to Marx, despite some difficult episodes in the short run, the world could look forward to a happy, classless society in which everyone would live in freedom and maximum personal fulfillment.

Professing Christians were not immune from this pervasive optimism, which profoundly affected and inspired proponents of the "social gospel"—men and women of expansive good will but doubtful theology, who believed that the chief mission of Christianity was to speed up this process of establishing a heaven on earth. In the United States, spiritual and materialistic values were confused in widespread talk about the great so-called American Christian Republic that would light the way to a glorious future.

In Defense of the Concept.   Before we contrast the cult of progress with a more genuinely Christian view of history, let us say a few words in defense of the cult.

The fact is, even though the blessings of modern science, technology and expanded production have been unevenly distributed, recent centuries *have* brought higher living standards and other welcome advantages to even the humble people of the West. We who take for granted comfortable homes, medical care, vacations, retirement benefits and a host of luxuries must remember that most of our ancestors lived in one-room, dirt-floor huts on the ragged edge of subsistence, subject to the ravages of famine and disease, with no chance for an education or much opportunity to learn about the world outside the narrow limits of their own villages. It would reflect base ingratitude on our part to sneer at the evidences of material progress that we enjoy.

Further, while noting the materialistic and non-Christian aura often surrounding the cult of progress, we must remember that the state churches of Europe (representing the only Christianity most people knew) were in many cases the apologists for despotic governments and selfish aristocracies.

These institutions deserved to be superseded by an order promoting greater freedom, social justice and other evidences of the cherished progress.

The Problems of Progress. Its merits notwithstanding, the cult of progress presents profound problems close to the heart of human experience as recorded in history. In the first place, it involves a subtle contempt for the past. It implies not only that people have improved their material environment over the years, but that we, the people of today, are superior to our counterparts of past centuries. We have gradually emerged from the brutal savagery and vicious treachery of the past to the more human and humane race of today. Does this portray an accurate picture of today's human scene? Does it do full justice to high points of moral rectitude and magnanimity in the past?

The cult of progress violates the fundamental historical fact of perpetual change. The very idea of progress implies progress toward some goal. When this goal of the perfect being in the perfect environment has been reached, what then? If change implies progress and progress has reached the ultimate, does time then stop?

Thus even amid the heady exuberance of nineteenth-century progress, the theory presented serious perplexities even to the secular scholar. But here we want to pay special attention to the implications of the theory for the Christian faith.

It may be true that Christianity habituated Westerners to look forward toward a bright day in the future. But Christian doctrine teaches us that humanity has been corrupted by sin and that our only hope lies in redemption through Christ's death and resurrection. The progress theory became increasingly popular as conviction of the fallen condition of humanity declined. This theory denies the fatal flaw in human nature, ignores life beyond the grave and substitutes a man-made utopia in this world for the heavenly city built by God for his people. In fact, does it not make the human race or possibly the processes of history a god?

World War 1 (1914-18) marks a great watershed between the confident optimism of the previous century and the pessimism of the twentieth. Perhaps your grandparents remember how the light of hope went out during those somber years. This century has witnessed two world wars, Communist and Fascist dictatorships, the horrors of the slave-labor camps, the threat of nuclear destruction and ominous environmental problems. The fact is that the idea of progress as an explanation of human history is just about dead.

The essential tragedy of the theory of progress is not that its dreams did not materialize, but that those dreams themselves were inadequate and partly false. Even when fulfilled they did not bring the happiness they seemed to promise.

A century ago, for instance, the future seemed to promise material abundance for all, an abundance that would dispel not only hunger but selfishness, hatred and crime. The moral flabbiness and deep unhappiness so often found in our affluent suburbs reveal the inadequacy of this dream. Progress in liberty promised the full development of each individual personality, but has just as often brought alienation from our fellows and deep loneliness. Democratic institutions were supposed to end the domination of the masses by oppressive governments, but modern totalitarian dictatorships have proved quite adept at using certain democratic processes for their own ends. The conquest of distance through modern transportation and communication was to unify the world into a great community, but instead has expanded local wars into catastrophes of worldwide scope. Conquest of nature has resulted in a tragic waste of limited natural resources, and the advance of human reason and the expansion of knowledge have produced devices and processes that can destroy the human race in a moment.

Once in a while we still hear historians whistling in the dark, expressing confidence that despite all appearances, somehow humanity will muddle through. But the whistling is only a faint echo of the crashing cymbals of progress heard only a century ago. With the demise of the cult of progress, secular history seems to have lost its sense of direction. What substitute does it offer now for the second coming of Christ and the heavenly city revealed in Scripture?

Marxism and Marxist History

Marxism is almost as difficult to define as the clouds drifting by overhead. Karl Marx (1818-83) and his collaborator Friedrich Engels (1820-95) were not themselves completely consistent. And their followers have displayed considerable divergence of thought. Some mechanically quote Marx in and out of context. Others twist his writings to suit their own purposes, often asking, "What would Marx say if he were alive today?" and then putting their own words in his mouth. (As one student said in frustration, "If Marx were alive today he would turn over in his grave!") Lenin, Stalin and Mao Tse-tung added their own corollaries in the light of concrete situations they faced.

To make matters even more difficult, the totalitarian Marxist regimes of the Soviet Union, mainland China and elsewhere all claim to be custodians of the true Marxist gospel, which they and their agents in the historical profession interpret and use as instruments of totalitarian control. When a historian is referred to as a Marxist, one must ask whether he is a Trotskyite, Stalinist, Maoist, Social Democratic revisionist or some other brand. In the West, many historians accept some features of Marxism while rejecting others.

The Marxist View of History. Behind these variations there is a core of Marxist doctrine which has profoundly affected the writings of orthodox Marxist historians everywhere. We have space here for only the barest skeleton of the doctrine as it affects the study of history. But because Marxism casts its shadow over so much of the world, it merits further study when you have opportunity.

To begin with, orthodox Marxism is anti-Christian from the center out. Marx was a thoroughgoing theoretical materialist, claiming that the basic reality is matter in motion, and denying the existence of God and the basically spiritual nature of man. He viewed history primarily in economic terms: human life and institutions all have an economic (that is, a material) base. He further taught that history moves forward as a result of the conflict of opposing economic forces, not in a straight line but in a zigzag movement.

More specifically, Marx claimed that the mode of production (such as hunting and fishing, farming or machine industry) and particularly the class which controls production, determines the nature of all human institutions ("economic determinism"). Thus government, education, family arrangements, art, literature and religion are all agencies of the ruling class to maintain itself in power. "Religion is the opiate of the people" (to keep them quiet in the face of oppression).[7]

Marx taught that the struggle between the exploiting ruling class and the exploited working masses is the basic element in history ("dialectical materialism"). In the past it had taken different forms—patrician versus slave, feudal lord versus serf. In modern industrial countries, the struggles continue between the bourgeoisie or capitalist class and the proletariat or propertyless working class. In the contemporary struggle, the proletariat was sure to win. It is this practice of interpreting almost all historical events (including such diverse developments as the Protestant Reformation and the American Civil War) in terms of class struggle that gives Marxist history its most distinctive characteristic.

But with the anticipated victory of the proletariat over the bourgeoisie, the Marxist theory of history takes a sharp turn. Instead of a resumption of the class struggle in a new form, Marx anticipated that now the proletariat would establish a temporary dictatorship, which would not only abolish private property but would establish a classless society. Logically, without classes there could not be any class struggle. And since government (as we have noted) has in past epochs been merely an agency of the ruling class to maintain itself in power, there would now no longer be any need for government. The end of the hatreds and turmoil and oppression of the past would be reached. Without oppressive government and other coercive institutions, the race could blossom amid the liberty of the perfect society. As mentioned in the previous section, Marxism is in effect a variant of the cult of progress.

Implications and Weaknesses. Now let us quickly summarize the main implications of the Marxist theory of history, many of which you have no doubt already sensed.

Christians, of course, are immediately antagonized by Marx's denial of God, of the truths of the Christian gospel, and of the primacy of the spirit. His system offers no supernatural support in trouble, no redemption from sin, no transcendent purpose to life, no hope beyond the grave. The primarily economic view of the past falls short of explaining either the thoughts and motives or the actions of human beings. The Marxist road—class hatred, bloodshed and dictatorship—could never lead to the land of promise that Marx described. One wonders whether it would be worth reaching—a world inhabited only by unregenerate people, without God or bond of Christian love.

Although the whole theory may seem highly imaginative to us, Marx believed that his view of history was thoroughly "scientific." He believed he had discovered the fundamental laws of historical development, as contrasted to the vague gropings of rival interpretations of the past. And this alleged discovery of "scientific laws" in turn implied that history *had* to develop in the way he described, just as knowledge of the law of gravitation enables us to anticipate what will happen when an object is dropped from a certain height. You will note, further, that little is said about individual human beings, their aspirations, frustrations, choices and responsibilities—an omission typical of deterministic systems.

Unfortunately for the strict Marxist, history has not vindicated Marx's vision of the future. Life in industrial capitalist countries, despite problems, has not dichotomized into two distinct and antagonistic economic classes. In Marxist lands there has been little progress toward a classless society, and the "temporary" dictatorship of the proletariat gives no evidence of surrendering its power. The secret state police and huge bureaucracies have been more symbolic of Marxist societies than the free and voluntary associations Marx anticipated.

Marxist historians traditionally reflect their mentor's bias against classes and institutions that meet with their disfavor. This includes, of course, the Christian community. But the class struggle is simply inadequate as an explanation of our highly complex past. There have been too many other factors involved. This overemphasis on economic antagonisms often leads the Marxist historian far afield. Trying to explain the Reformation, the Counter Reformation, the Puritans or the eighteenth-century Great Awakening in primarily economic terms is like selling Rembrandt paintings by the pound.

Some Favorable Effects. In fairness, however, Christians must recognize that Marxism has had some favorable effects on the study and writing of history.

Marx reminds us, for instance, that one situation in history rarely develops out of another in a straight line of cause and effect. What has happened has frequently been a result of clashing interests, including those of economic classes.

Further, before the advent of Marxism, historians no doubt paid far *too little* attention to economics. Marx was surely right when he wrote that unless we make a living, we will not be around to do anything else. Historians have too often concentrated on the sleazy plots and intrigues of courtiers and courtesans, as if these were the essential stuff of the human experience. Decisions in chancelleries and parliaments, maneuvers of armies and navies and production of artistic and literary masterpieces all involve economic resources, a fact easily forgotten.

Moreover, Marxist historians have made a helpful contribution in their emphasis on the lower classes. Because of the scarcity of documentary sources, or perhaps because of bias in favor of the rich and powerful, historians have often neglected the lives and aspirations of the poor and lowly. Christian students and teachers of history, especially, need to be sensitive on this point. Marx himself was at his best when he, like an Old Testament prophet, denounced the selfishness and callous indifference of establishment types of his day. We sometimes have cause to suspect the motivation behind Marxist patronage of the downtrodden, but it is still true that Marxists have shown concern for the material well-being of their fellows, though perhaps not recognizing the source of such values.

Still, in its essential form, orthodox Marxism is so completely incompatible with authentic Christianity that an accommodation between the two requires denial of basic features of Marxism or Christianity or both.

Tool of the Totalitarian State
So far we have said little about the totalitarian use or (more accurately) abuse of history. Many groups publish works of history for publicity or propaganda purposes. The aim might be to vindicate the group or its leaders, answer criticisms or attract adherents. Their main weakness is usually their onesidedness; they do not tell the whole story. In most cases, however, we can find other works that give the opposing point of view. By perusing works representing both sides we

can usually get a fairly well-balanced picture.

A good example of this type of situation is the "battle of the books" following the Reformation. Protestants published the *Magdeburg Centuries,* Roman Catholics the *Ecclesiastical Annals.* Both were highly partisan, but between them they covered most of the ground in dispute. If both sides had been as Christian as they claimed to be, they would have produced fairer and more candid works. But at least the avid searcher for truth had opportunity to find it.

The situation is quite different in totalitarian regimes. Here the purpose is mind control—to produce subjects whose mental processes have been shaped by the regime. Education becomes indoctrination. Using sophisticated modern communication techniques, the regime feeds the people a carefully concocted diet of information and misinformation designed to produce mechanical backers of the state. All histories favor the system; unfavorable works are banned or burned.

You can imagine the kind of history such a situation produces. Historians are not free agents describing the past as they see it as a result of objective research. They are, instead, part of the propaganda apparatus of the regime. Facts about the past are carefully selected and usually distorted to serve the state's purposes. Since the regime controls all the means of communication (books, magazines, newspapers, scholarly journals, radio, television) and excludes all opposing points of view, readers or listeners have no basis of comparison and even against their own inclinations find their thinking processes succumbing to the regime's control.

Among the most chilling scenes from Nazi Germany are the movies of German students committing intellectual suicide at a great book-burning festival in Berlin.[8] Describing the situation in the Soviet Union, Alexander Solzhenitsyn had to say sadly that only the West knew the true history of his country—his own people did not.

So-called Christian regimes down through the years have also endeavored to exercise thought control. But they did so in direct contradiction of the teaching of Scripture, which emphasizes from beginning to end that liberty of conscience and freedom of choice are essential to our stature as human beings.

Every totalitarian regime must take special pains to control the writing and teaching of history because our view of the past experience of the human race to a large extent determines our outlook on all of life. In a way, totalitarian abuse of history is in essence a theory of history. The authority of the state becomes the highest good; history is merely another of the tools used to enhance that power. This emerges as just another variety of idolatry.

When studying the fall of the Roman Empire or the outbreak of the French Revolution or the performance of the American "New Deal," you may find that, in each case, six historians explain these events in half a dozen different, and perhaps contradictory, ways. You may be tempted to throw up your hands and shout in frustration, "Why don't the historians get together and give me the straight scoop? I'm completely befuddled!"

When this happens, remember that we could be living in a time and place where the "straight scoop" is the propaganda line of the state and proponents of other views end up in prison camps.

No Golden Key
We have discussed representative ways in which historians have endeavored to explain the past experience of the human race. You will have noted that from a Christian perspective most have both strengths and weaknesses. Almost all of them contribute something to a right understanding of the past; none supplies the golden key that unlocks its full meaning.

As you pursue your history studies you will find it profitable to look for examples of these suggested patterns of the past. Is the author you are reading an exponent of one or another of these schools? Do the facts presented argue in favor of any of them, or do they cast doubt on their validity? What Christian truths help you in forming your judgments?

Christian Faith and Understanding the Past

5

In this chapter we will look at some distinguishing characteristics of the Christian faith which should help us in our study of the past. Then we will consider dangers or pitfalls that have trapped unwary Christians in the tangled forest of history.

In the Image of God

First of all, the distinctive Christian view that human beings are created in the image of God makes the study of human experience more vivid, meaningful and crucial. Since every individual is a spiritual as well as a biological being with eternal life to gain or lose, we believe that every actor in the historical drama is deeply significant and important.[1]

Various non-Christian systems of explaining the past have made human beings mere means to certain "higher" ends—cogs in huge machines grinding out historical events. Some historians have claimed that the state is the essential element of history. Hitler's Nazis lumped all individual personalities into the category of "Volk," while orthodox Marxists lump them into social classes such as the "bourgeoisie" or the "proletariat." Christians have sometimes yielded to temptations to depersonalize human beings, but sooner or later they are stopped short by the plain teachings of the gospel.

If we are true to our faith, we will feel a deep compassion for the people we are studying—a compassion that helps us share their feelings, triumphs and frustrations. This ability to involve ourselves in the experiences of other people is one of the most important aids to understanding the past. We must not believe that Christians are the only ones who can so empathize with people in history. But Christians have a very special reason for empathizing, believing as we do that they were all human beings for whom our Savior died. It is sometimes difficult to convince students that men and women in the history text were actually genuine, bona fide human beings who had colds, naps, griefs, babies, doubts, plans, grandmothers and favorite foods just as people do today. We cannot truly get inside the characters we study about, but the effort to "walk in their shoes" will make the past more alive and real.

For example, when we try to identify so thoroughly with the participants in a historical event that we see the situation with their eyes, we will realize that none of them could foretell the future. They had no way of knowing, as we do now, what would be the long-range effects of their actions. In his 1938 negotiations with Adolf Hitler, Neville Chamberlain did not know that appeasement would lead to war. He believed that policy to be the best way to keep the peace.

The Bible emphasizes that this concern and compassion must extend to all, not merely to people of our own race, nation or group. Jesus warned against the narrow parochialism that was so prevalent even among his own followers (Lk.

4:24-27). And it took a rather spectacular vision to convince Peter that "God shows no partiality, but in every nation any one who fears him and does what is right is acceptable to him" (Acts 10:34-35).

Such open-mindedness toward people of diverse races, nationalities and cultures is absolutely essential to a proper appreciation of the past. Interest in world missions has at least partially opened the eyes of Christians to the worth of people of other continents and cultures. On the other hand, if we had been more faithful to the Christian ideals we profess, we would not have waited for secular scholars to assume much of the initiative in giving credit to the role of blacks, Indians, Chicanos and other minorities in American history.

The Christian also has the advantage of the Bible's profound and unvarnished portrait of human character—deeply sympathetic but without illusion. The Scriptures teach us that human beings are capable of the noblest virtue, but also of the vilest crimes. Remember David, the sensitive hero whose rectitude would not allow him to harm Saul even when the king sought his life? This same David ordered the murder of a good man to hide his own sin of adultery. We should not be unduly disillusioned by history's accounts of human perfidy and corruption since the Bible tells us that the human "heart is deceitful above all things, and desperately corrupt" (Jer. 17:9), the cause of all sorts of misery. On the other hand, the Bible also teaches that human beings are redeemable and gives many examples of personalities transformed by God's grace. Over and over again history vindicates this biblical picture of the human race.

We will be greatly helped in our study of the men and women of history if we keep before us this biblical picture of humanity created in the image of God, endowed with the power and responsibility of moral choice, fallen but redeemable. And if we are appalled by human deceitfulness, we always come back to the awkward question, Would I have done better?

The Whole Pertinent Truth

Another distinct characteristic of the Christian faith which should help in the study of history is its insistence on absolute truthfulness. As intimated previously, acceptance of the lordship of Christ should be the strongest possible sanction for the most meticulous honesty. The Christian should be characterized not only by conventional honesty in the sense of avoiding outright falsehood, but by honesty in the full sense of "the truth, the whole truth, and nothing but the truth"—no evasion or subterfuge of any kind.

The fact that some Christians have not been altogether truthful in the past merely shows that they have fallen short of the clear standards of Christ. It should not obscure the fact that the Christian is under the strictest mandate to avoid falsehood in any form. The Bible is replete with examples to illustrate the point, condemning even its greatest heroes from Abraham to the Apostle Peter when they weaseled or dissembled in any way.

The true Christian genuinely believes that Christ is the truth as well as the way and the life. We may expect all kinds of charges to be leveled against Christians and the institutional church (many of them for good reason), but these are not the objects of our faith. We know that no fault can be found in Christ. Thus we need not fear that some inconvenient fact will show up to wreck the Christian faith. Every believer, whether a historian writing history or a student enrolled in a history course, will want to know the whole pertinent truth. Mature, accurate judgments about the meaning of the human experience cannot be formed on the basis of half truths or distortions. "You will know the truth, and the truth will make you free" (Jn. 8:32).

Value Judgments

Another contribution of the Christian faith to the study of history lies in the area of value judgments. When Jesus said, "Judge not, that you be not judged" (Mt. 7:1), he did not mean that we should avoid forming opinions of others or that we should not condemn what we know to be wrong. He was warning his followers against censoriousness or taking delight in unfavorable and unkind criticism.[2] Judging, in the sense of evaluating and discriminating between wisdom and folly and between right and wrong, is the mark of our stature as intelligent and moral beings endowed with the responsibility of making choices. Every time we exercise that responsibility—when we choose our friends, when we decide how to use our time, when we vote for candidates for office, when we agree or disagree with statements of our pastors and professors, certainly when we decide whether to serve God or self—we make a value judgment. Some of these choices involve matters of personal taste; some concern the relative wisdom of alternative courses of action; some raise basic questions of right and wrong.[3]

If we really think about the activities of men and women in history we constantly make value judgments. Frequently we do this subconsciously. Did Caesar act wisely and morally when he decided to cross the Rubicon? Did the crusaders act virtuously when they captured Jerusalem? Was Martin Luther right to challenge the authority of the Pope? Were the pilgrims wise when they left the Old World to endure the rigors of the New? Should President Ford have pardoned his predecessor?

Fortunately, we have both the privilege and the responsibility to withhold judgment when the evidence before us is insufficient, as it so often is. But we have to ask ourselves at what point withholding judgment is merely indifference or lack of moral sensitivity.

In making our value judgments we naturally must have

some criterion, some scale by which we measure relative wisdom or virtue. There are many such scales. Possibly the most common is a feeling for what is approved by the society around us. As Christians we have the great advantage of a God-given standard—the teaching of Scripture confirmed by a conscience enlightened by the Holy Spirit. For instance, in evaluating the career of Napoleon Bonaparte, the Christian student will doubtless approve some of the emperor's policies for the reconstruction of France after years of confusion, but condemn his many violations of the Bible's injunctions against pride and hunger for power.

Distinctively Christian Values

Immediately questions arise. In the first place, are distinctively Christian choices confined to the moral and spiritual spheres? Is there a Christian mathematics as well as Christian mathematicians, Christian physics as well as Christian physicists? Or does the issue boil down to the question of whether or not these disciplines are used for God-approved purposes?

This is an important consideration because there are so many questions in political theory, economics and public policy, for example, where Christians legitimately differ. Sincere followers of Christ do not always agree on the meaning and application of Scripture, and the "Christian conscience" is a very personal, individual thing. We want to be careful about calling people unchristian because they disagree with us on such matters. People have a tendency to muddy the waters by slapping the adjective *Christian* on all kinds of ideas and movements that in reality are neutral (spiritually speaking) or reflect human aspirations rather than the purposes of God.

You may recall learning in a United States history class that in the 1890s articulate enthusiasts tried to wage a veritable spiritual crusade for the "free and unlimited coinage of silver at the ratio of sixteen to one." This was to be the cure for all our country's ills. To support "free silver" was a Christian duty; to oppose it was to be a tool of Satan's minions. At various times sincere people have insisted that all true Christians must support the Democratic Party, while others have just as vociferously insisted that all Christians must vote Republican. We do not argue here that Christians should not support "free silver," or the Democratic Party, or the Republican Party, if they believe this would promote the general welfare. What we must object to is identifying any cause with the cause of Christ unless clear-cut spiritual or moral issues are involved.

Despite such legitimate reservations, there is such a thing as a Christian system of values and morality, and there is a distinctively Christian approach to the study of history. On many, many matters the Scriptures are so clear and positive and the witness of Christians has been so nearly unanimous that the appellation *Christian* is entirely appropriate. The majesty of God, our creation in his image, our responsibility to him in thought and action, our duty to abide by a moral code divinely established for human happiness, our recognition of the tragic consequences of disobedience to that law, God's offer of redemption and eternal life through faith in Christ, the primacy of love toward God and our neighbor—such beliefs are clearly Christian and give Jesus' followers a uniquely Christian outlook. This outlook will naturally affect their value judgments about people, manners and movements in history.

Let me illustrate. Most people (including historians) have in the back of their minds a picture, clear or fuzzy, of an ideal society abounding in justice and human happiness. Against this they compare an actual society of yesterday or today. On the basis of such a model, we judge one proposed policy to be better than another. Just about everybody will agree that in such an ideal society there will be a reasonable degree of material well-being for all. Most would also agree that such a society should be intellectually alive and should guarantee the liberty that enables individuals to develop their potential to the full. It might also be agreed that such a society ought to promote a sense of community and brotherhood.

Christians accept all such elements as thoroughly consistent with our mental picture of what God wants his creatures to enjoy. But we cannot stop here, as some do, for a supremely necessary component is missing—the spiritual. In the ideal society, everyone, young and old, will live in vital and intimate fellowship with God and in joyful obedience to his commands, will grow spiritually as well as physically and intellectually. Christians do not believe that such a society will ever actually materialize here on earth, but something like this is the model of perfection against which we measure the actual scenes of history.

Recognizing a Historian's Values
When we read a historical work, therefore, we should try to determine the author's standard of values. We cannot adequately understand the implications of the work unless we do this. It will require a good deal of concentration. We will have to think analytically about the material we are studying. We will probably have to read between the lines because writers rarely state their values explicitly.

Frequently a historian betrays his or her values by chance remarks, by the amount of space devoted to a given theme or by the nuances of the language. Sometimes we discern the author's values by a subtle tone pervading a work. Often we can catch hints of the historian's values by learning something about his background. This method is not infallible, however, since historians of similar backgrounds may cherish widely divergent values.

Economic Factors.   If a historian gives the most space to discussing the gross national product, balance of payments, income distribution and the price structure, he may be either writing an economic history (certainly a legitimate field) or implying that economic success and material comfort are the highest good. If there is a strong emphasis on class conflict and "the good of the revolution," you are probably reading a Marxist historian.

Human Achievement.   Other writers prize above all else human achievements in the fine arts and other enterprises. They are strongly humanistic in their enthusiasm for the outward reach of the human spirit as expressed by painters, sculptors, architects, authors, philosophers, theoretical scientists and explorers by land, sea and air. Naturally, they highly esteem the Renaissance period, some claiming that the Reformation was a step backward because it turned people's thoughts back to religion in place of the man-centered achievements of geniuses such as Leonardo da Vinci and Benvenuto Cellini. This basis of values is clearly seen in the works of Voltaire, for example, who saw four "blessed ages" when "the arts were perfected"—the Athens of Pericles (fifth century B.C.), the Rome of Julius Caesar (first century B.C.), the Italy of the Medici (fourteenth century) and the France of Louis XIV (seventeenth century).

The Nation-State.   Still other historians (most notably in the nineteenth century) inferred, if they did not baldly state, that the power and glory of the nation-state are the highest good. They idolized the virtues of their own nation and the valor and "world mission" of its people. They admired military strength and other forms of national power. This tendency reached its peak among German historians such as Heinrich von Treitschke, but other countries, including the United States, also had their supernationalistic historians. You may run across the works of other, less partisan, writers who bestow the laurel wreath on whoever is successful in the use (or abuse) of power. The losers, regardless of virtue or courage, are tossed into the "ash can of history." The role of values here is quite obvious.

Liberty and Democracy. Nineteenth-century writers also produced a great deal of history which made liberty and representative government the touchstone by which all developments were measured. By *liberty* these historians meant either political and religious liberty or economic liberty (free enterprise or laissez faire) or both. These historians not only considered freedom the highest good, but made the advance of human liberty and constitutional government the keys to progress (see chapter four). Socialist historians, on the other hand, tend to believe that social and economic equality is a higher value than freedom.

Dramatic Effect. The books on the history shelves of your college library almost invariably deal with historical issues in a serious manner. But occasionally you will find a book that appeals primarily to those with a taste for the bizarre or sensational rather than for truth. Such books are, of course, usually meant to entertain. But at the same time they display a tawdry sense of values. The facts of history *are* sometimes curious or dramatic. The historian does not need to manufacture such scenes nor to unduly emphasize them to make an interesting story. Warm human sympathy, a feel for the basic issues confronting the participants and felicity of language are qualities that produce history which can be a delight to read as well as a contribution to the reader's understanding of human experience.

These five categories are, of course, only examples of the kinds of value systems that historians exhibit in their works. It is up to each of us to determine whether or not particular values are consistent or inconsistent with a Christian standard of values, or whether it is a question of priority or proportion. Conversely, we might ask ourselves to what extent our own standard of values may be influenced by what we learn about human personality and behavior through studying history.

Spiritual Elements of the Past

Have you ever stopped to think what an important advantage your own Christian experience gives you in understanding certain elements of the past? Sermons by our pastors, lessons of church-school teachers, rap sessions with Christian friends and especially our private reading of the Scriptures and Christian books give us a large store of information and insights that have surprising applicability in the study of history. Add to this such Christian experiences as peace with God and the thrill of answered prayer (experiences we share with countless people of past generations), and we have resources for understanding spiritual elements of history that the average college student lacks

Christianity from the Inside. Regardless of religious orientation, students of history have to recognize that Christianity has played a crucial role in the world for nearly two thousand years, particularly in the West. We do not claim that non-Christians are necessarily ignorant of this role. In fact, some non-Christian scholars have a remarkable knowledge of the nuances of Christian doctrine. Nevertheless, people who can view the Christian faith from the inside, so to speak, enjoy some advantages here. They have a fund of information concerning Christian doctrine and practice that the average non-Christian student usually has had little opportunity to obtain and a "feel" for Christian life and experience that the stranger to Christ cannot muster. Christian students can more easily identify with the feelings and outlook of people from the past who shared their Christian faith.

The Bible in Intellectual History. Furthermore, history students steeped in the Bible and Christian doctrine enjoy a clear advantage in understanding the intellectual history of the West as represented, for example, in imaginative literature. This is because the works of scholars and authors representing many different national cultures very frequently involve biblical themes and contain biblical images which

Christian students may more readily recognize. The forbidden fruit, the mark of Cain, the age of Methuselah, Nimrod the mighty hunter, Noah and the ark, the tower of Babel, the destruction of Sodom, Joseph and the coat of many colors are a few images from just one book, Genesis, that often appear in Western literature and would be poorly understood apart from a knowledge of the Bible. It is a mistake to think of such expressions as mere figures of speech. They represent a common biblical heritage that has given Western civilization much of the cohesion it has enjoyed for at least a millennium.

A "Christian" Civilization. Western civilization has been called "Christian" since the days of the Roman Empire, not because a majority of its people have been Christian in any genuine sense or because its institutions have necessarily reflected Christian principles, but because its basic presuppositions have been based in large part on a Christian view of God and humanity.

Until recently, most people in Europe and in societies emanating from Europe at least formally believed that the God of the Bible is the Creator of all things, that human beings are his special creation and responsible to him, that Christ is the redeemer of our fallen race, that the church is the visible body of Christ on earth, and that a judgment day is coming. Even when violating Christian standards and incurring God's wrath, people in the West have generally accepted this picture of the universe as valid. When professing Christians have quarreled over doctrine, they usually have not questioned the validity of these fundamental beliefs but only argued over who has best reflected them.

Such a view of God, mankind and the world comes as second nature to the Christian student of history. When we read about St. Francis of Assisi renouncing wealth and social position to walk in the footsteps of Christ or about the Puritans seeking a Zion in the North American wilderness or about Stonewall Jackson on his knees praying before a battle, a responsive chord is struck in our own hearts.

But consider the problem of students to whom such concepts are foreign. They have difficulty understanding what motivates people who cherish Christian beliefs. Frequently they cannot grasp what religious controversies are all about and are apt to dismiss them as perverse or inconsequential. Often through ignorance they accept as genuine what is only an insipid or burlesque caricature of the Christian faith. The following, for example, is the *total* description of the birth of Christianity in a high-school history text:

> Rome conquered Palestine in 63 B.C. While Rome governed the land, Jesus of Nazareth, who had been a simple carpenter, began a religious ministry among the Jews. He created such turmoil that about 30 A.D. the Roman governor had Him crucified. After His death, His disciples spread His teachings. Within one hundred years, many Mediterranean people had been converted to the new faith.[4]

There is no mention of the Christian's claim that Jesus is the Son of God, that he died to save fallen humanity, that he rose again and is alive today. Can you imagine the handicap suffered by a young person trying to understand the role of Christianity in history with such an anemic concept of what the Christian faith involves?

When ancient civilization collapsed in the West with the fall of the Roman Empire, the Christian church (though in imperfect form) was the only major institution to survive. Consequently, the church was the most important institution in Europe during the thousand-year formative period we call the Middle Ages. The Renaissance had a larger religious content than some of its enthusiasts have realized. Issues incident to the Protestant Reformation were at the heart of European history for more than a century. Christianity was often the most powerful force behind the emigration of Europeans to America and elsewhere. Modern science was born in an intellectual climate present only in the Christian (or, more accurately, semi-Christian) world. We could go on, but this is probably enough to validate the point that no one can hope to understand the history of the West while ignoring the role of the Christian religion. And who understands the inner reality of that religion as well as the Christian?

Because the Christian faith has little place in their own personal lives, many professional historians frequently minimize the role of Christianity in their writing or teaching. For instance, one of the most popular modern European history texts used in our colleges and universities dismisses the eighteenth-century Methodist revival in six words ("the Methodist movement began in England"). It does not even mention John Wesley, despite the profound effect of Methodism on eighteenth-century England and its continuing influence since that time.[5]

In the case of public-school history textbooks, the problem undoubtedly stems in part from an exaggerated concept of the separation of church and state. Textbook writers hope to avoid hassles by almost entirely eliminating the role of religion, even though this gives pupils the mistaken idea that religion has not been very important in the human experience. Students fail to learn about the role of Christianity in the struggle against evils such as slavery and child labor or the part Christian faith has played in inspiring artists, writers and musicians. Compare, for example, the light treatment given the Christian religion in most American history textbooks with the leading and dynamic role ascribed to it by Yale Professor Sydney E. Ahlstrom in his *A Religious History of the American People*. Dr. Ahlstrom, whose references to evangelical Christianity are not always favorable, emphasizes so strongly its role in America's early development that he refers to it as a "quasi-establishment" in the United States:

As the great revivals followed one after the other, a quasi-

establishment of evangelical Protestantism emerged. Not even the great antebellum sectional controversy interfered with its progress, because evangelicalism deepened its hold in both the North and the South.[6]
When they do write or lecture about the role of religion, secular historians are usually factually correct in dealing with its outward manifestations, but typically fail to grasp the inward feelings and thoughts of the people they describe. The Christian historian and teacher should be able to treat these subtle and inward aspects more sensitively.

Kenneth Scott Latourette, an eminent Christian historian, was one who saw that the historical profession had largely ignored the important subject of Christian missions in the Far East, and applied himself to the task of rectifying this serious omission.[7] In the process he corrected another common historical error. Historians had generally maintained that the nineteenth century was a time of retreat for Christianity as the traditional faith was challenged by the cult of science, Marxism, supernationalism and a pervasive materialism. Latourette showed that, looking at the larger world scene, Christianity was actually advancing as missionaries brought the gospel to the four corners of the earth.

The Tyranny of Relevance
The Christian faith guards the student against the tyranny of mislabeled relevance. When told that education must be relevant, the first question to ask is: Relevant to what? We must insist that history be relevant not to the narrow preoccupations of the existing moment nor to some ephemeral fad of the historical popularizers, but to the real issues of life.

Of course, we must not stretch this point too far. History *should* illuminate the problems of our own day. As we have pointed out before, one of its valuable uses is to show the antecedents of various features of today's world. But, on the other hand, we do not want to absorb ourselves so completely in the confining concerns of the present moment that we lock ourselves in a prison marked "Today" and lose sight of the enduring questions. If we do, we will fail to prepare ourselves to meet new problems as they arise.

The Christian faith, with its concentration on values of lasting importance, applicable everywhere and for all time, should help us take this longer view.

Finally, the Bible teaches and the experience of Christians through the centuries confirms that the Holy Spirit in response to faith illuminates the mind of the believer, bringing insights that reason alone could not discern. Some might call this simply intuition; we know it is the work of God. In answer to prayer the Holy Spirit can illuminate for us the significant lessons behind the facts we learn. But this can never substitute for diligent study nor compensate for failure to do adequate research.

Snags and Snares

Up to this point, we have noted the advantages Christians enjoy, or should enjoy, in their effort to understand the past. These advantages are based on Christianity's view of humanity, its high regard for truth, the quality of its value structure and its sensitivity to the spiritual component of history.

These advantages should result in a grasp of the human experience that enriches our lives and increases our understanding of current issues. In actual practice, however, these advantages have far too often been only potential. The sad fact is that Christians sometimes fail to utilize their advantages in understanding the past. Let's take a look at some of the pitfalls to be avoided.

Egocentricity
Earlier we discussed the typically Christian concern for each

human being and the individual's key role in the pageant of history. This concern is emphatically biblical, as a study of the Scriptures will amply illustrate. But there is a danger of carrying this emphasis beyond what the Scriptures teach and claiming that nonpersonal factors have no place in history at all.

It is manifestly impossible to describe the past in solely personal terms; there are too many people to be able to deal with each individually. Of course, when we discuss institutions such as the state, school or church we have to remember that these are abstractions. The reality lies in the individual people composing them, each with his or her own unique personality. But these terms are a very convenient system of shorthand we use to make possible a narrative involving large groups of people.

When describing a presidential election, for instance, it is impossible for the historian to discuss how each individual voted. And it is obviously legitimate for the observer to use statistical means, perhaps a computer, to generalize about the voting behavior of various categories of people, such as Catholics, blacks, young people, white-collar workers or labor-union members. Such categorizing can lead to useful conclusions. But all the time we must recognize the hazards involved in all generalizations. And we must remember that a person is an individual first and a member of a group second.

Institutions are important because they are the repositories of interests and values held in common by the members of the group. We make a sad mistake if we fail to recognize the importance of the factors that bind human beings together in communities. The egocentricity that makes the individual the center of a tight little personal world with no outside responsibilities is highly undesirable.

Also, material factors such as economics and geography are often of crucial importance because they describe the milieu and set the limits within which individuals operate. How can we avoid the conclusion that climate and other geographic factors help explain why highly vigorous civilizations have usually (not always) developed in temperate zones rather than in tropical areas or frozen polar regions? Economic factors are important simply because it is necessary to make a living in order to survive. Moreover, in our own experience have we not noticed that a desire for wealth is a powerful motive?

The Bible clearly recognizes the critical influence of economic factors, as witnessed by the various provisions of the Mosaic Law discouraging concentrations of great wealth and an excessively wide gulf between rich and poor. The writer of Proverbs 30 understood this clearly:

Remove far from me falsehood and lying;
> give me neither poverty nor riches;
> feed me with the food that is needful for me,
lest I be full, and deny thee,
> and say, "Who is the LORD?"
or lest I be poor, and steal,
> and profane the name of my God. (Prov. 30:8-9)

Is there possibly a connection between the fabulous economic prosperity of Solomon's reign, when silver was "as common in Jerusalem as stone" (1 Kings 10:27), and the picture of sexual license described in Proverbs 7?

Christians certainly have no quarrel with economic and other environmental explanations of human developments so long as they are confined to describing the perimeters within which individuals can make choices. These explanations should not brush aside human beings as mere parts of the stage furniture.

Trifling with the Truth
Despite the Scriptures' emphatic insistence in precept and example on scrupulous truthfulness and fairness, Christians

all too frequently disseminate misinformation.

Some of this mischief can be explained by pointing out that the guilty parties were not, or are not, Christians at all. Many people parade under the name *Christian* who are not in any meaningful way Jesus' followers and certainly do not have the mind of Christ. Since we find such charlatans in every other area of life, it is only reasonable to expect them in the history field as well. For example, in spite of the fact that the Nazism of the 1930s and '40s ran counter to everything that Christ stands for, some pseudohistorians espoused this vicious ideology in the name of Christianity.

Even today there are some who propagate as a true document *The Protocols of the Learned Elders of Zion*, a notorious forgery purporting to outline a Jewish plan to dominate the world.[1] These people look to some form of Neo-Nazism to "save" Christianity. Since those who disseminate such falsehoods in no way reflect a true Christian position, their machinations should not affect the Christian's reputation for truthfulness.

But we cannot blame this whole problem on pseudo-Christians. Other, more genuine, Christians have too often perpetuated historical error, though for less vicious reasons. Sometimes the problem is simple carelessness. Christians hear or read an interesting bit of information and pass it on without checking its source or making any effort to check its accuracy. Probably some of this is inevitable. We are not all trained scholars and cannot be expected to recognize every error. Nor do we have the time to do extensive research on every piece of information we pass along. But sometimes are we not a little too trusting or gullible? Should we not be more careful of the "facts" we pass on? Before we accept a statement as true, the very least we should do is ask, Is the source of this information reliable? Is the writer or speaker knowledgeable in the area in question, whether science, economics, politics, international affairs or any other field? Does he or she have access to the facts? We who presume to teach or write history have a very special responsibility to thoroughly check not only our facts but our conclusions.

A particularly strong temptation to distort history confronts the historian who writes about an institution or movement to which he or she has a personal emotional attachment or antipathy. The historian must constantly ask, Am I being completely fair or am I allowing my personal feelings unduly to color my work? We say *unduly* because we cannot object to a historian expressing personal convictions or loyalties. But these should not be an excuse for painting a false picture.

Another type of distortion is represented by Christian writers who depict their own nation as the "People of God." Ignoring the seamier side of its history, they tell us that their nation basks under the special, and perhaps exclusive, approval of God. This approach reached some kind of apogee around the turn of the twentieth century in the writings of the Reverend Josiah Strong, who claimed that the United States had a divinely ordained mission to "Anglo-Saxonize" the world in the interest of the purest Christianity.[2] On the other hand are the supercritics who, in professed loyalty to the highest Christian ideals, fail to show any charity toward either their country or its leaders, as they face serious practical problems in dealing with the world situation.

Do Evil That Good May Come
Is it legitimate for a Christian historian (or any other Christian) to distort the truth if this promises to advance the cause of Christ? The answer from Scripture is a thunderous, No! (See Rom. 3:8.) As we have mentioned before, we grossly insult Christ's holy cause if we imply that it needs to be propped up by any kind of falsehood. The record of human experience illustrates over and over again the disastrous moral results of attempting to defeat one evil by embracing

another. If Christianity is genuinely, not superficially, valid, we should be able to face *all* the facts, not merely the ones that appear favorable. We need to remember always that it is Christ we worship, not an institution or a movement or Christian people, no matter how great or noble.

But although we deny in theory that the end justifies the means, in practice Christian authors and lecturers (and probably you and I) sometimes do the opposite. Not that we often tell barefaced lies—we are too moral for that. But in more subtle ways we are tempted to manipulate the truth to make it serve our purposes. The more zealous we are to serve Christ's cause, the stronger this temptation can be unless we are thoroughly imbued with the mind of Christ.

This manipulation of the facts can take any number of different forms. We can omit significant facts that would change the complexion of the story. We can concentrate heavily on one set of facts at the expense of others just as pertinent. We can fail to explain background factors that would make an act appear more rational. We can give the impression that conjecture is proven fact. We can state unusual facts and give the impression they are typical. We can excuse men and women with whom we identify ("There were extenuating circumstances" or "They were merely following the standard of their own times"), while making no such concessions for their opponents. We can compare the best representatives of one side with the worst of the other side, instead of comparing best with best and worst with worst.

For instance, a Protestant historian narrating the story of the Reformation might compare Martin Luther with the worldly Pope Leo X rather than with Luther's friend Johannes Staupitz, an earnest and warm-hearted monk who chose to remain within the Church. Incidentally, in so doing the historian would neglect treating an important dilemma. Sincere sixteenth-century Christians struggled with themselves and with fellow believers over whether to join the Reformers or to remain loyal to their own Church.

It is no defense to argue that it is standard practice in our society to tell only one side of a story. The point is that Christians should not follow the standard practices of society but those of Christ.

A great deal is at stake here. When historians falsify the picture of the past in any way, they make it more difficult for their readers or listeners to face reality and thus form sound judgments. Facts and ideas are the building blocks of our whole structure of thought. Even "small" falsehoods can so weaken the structure that it cannot stand the stress of criticism. And any kind of distortion reflects not only on ourselves but on the reputation and integrity of Christ's cause in the world. The lesson here is certainly plain. Although the odds against complete, transparent honesty are great, the Christian historian and history student can be satisfied with nothing less.

Credulity

Faith and credulity are not the same. Credulity—a disposition to believe too readily—is another serious pitfall in the study of history. It is well illustrated by a great deal of the history written during the so-called Dark Ages, the three or four centuries following the collapse of the Roman Empire in the West. During this unhappy time much of the knowledge and many of the methods of scholarship known to antiquity were lost. Such knowledge as did survive in Western Europe was kept alive almost solely by Christian monks, many in isolated monasteries far from the centers of classical civilization. Without their dedicated labors, the world would be infinitely poorer today. But even these monks, almost the only scholars left, suffered from the ignorance and credulity of the time. A characteristic of their scholarship was a very common tendency to see miracles and saintly wonders everywhere.

For example, St. Gregory of Tours, a sixth-century bishop and historian, was one of the best scholars of his day. Without his *History of the Franks* our knowledge of sixth-century Gaul would be far more defective than it is now. But, as is copiously illustrated by his fascinating *Eight Books of Miracles*, he was typical of the few educated people of his day in his boundless faith in religious relics. He tells us that his mother wore around her neck a small gold case containing the ashes of certain saints. Once when a great fire was destroying the crops in her neighborhood, she lifted up these holy relics and the fire went out in a moment. When Gregory was ill with dysentery and high fever, he was reportedly cured by drinking a mixture of water and dust from the tomb of St. Martin. He tells many such stories, all typical of the thought of that time.

Although as Christians we believe God can and does work miracles, we cannot help but be a little skeptical of such stories, especially since the alleged miracles were said to take place almost constantly. But the point here is that these writers were honest and sincere men who were only reflecting the credulity of their age. They recorded what they thought they saw, uncorrected by modern methods of critical scholarship. It may be true, however, that with the eye of faith they had a vision of the unseen world that today's critical scholars lack. Nevertheless, our faith in God's power to work miracles does not excuse us from checking our facts when we claim that supernatural factors have been at work. There is a fine line between credulity and faith, and as educated Christians it is our duty to find it.

Casting Stones
Now let us take a look at our Christian standard of values from another vantage point. As Christians we believe that values taught by Scripture are absolute and thus valid for all time, everywhere. We need to think very seriously about

what these absolutes are in the area of human conduct. Are they confined to the Ten Commandments? the Sermon on the Mount? the golden rule? What is the role of conscience? Whose authority do we accept with respect to interpretation of biblical commands? These are not questions we can answer here, but they must be faced by everyone who wants to evaluate historical figures and events according to Christian standards.

Those who study people representing widely divergent cultures with widely divergent moral codes face the grave danger of drifting into philosophical relativism—the idea that truth and morality are relative to individuals and the times and places in which they act. We must recognize this as a profoundly non-Christian stance. It gives to human beings the right to establish basic standards, a right belonging to God alone. It denies or ignores the biblical teaching that entire cultures can adopt and practice false standards (Rom. 1:21-32).

On the other hand, even though we firmly believe that God's standards are absolute and unchanging, simple justice impels us, when bringing an individual before the bar of history, to take into consideration his or her environment and culture. David's polygamy, for example, must be considered in terms of the customs of his day. People who live in primitive villages may be excused for displaying less refinement in speech and manner than a nobleman at the king's court. A new Christian, converted out of a totally pagan environment, cannot be blamed if remnants of old ideas and practices are slow in dissolving.

In fact, the more we think about the human dilemma, the slower we will be to condemn. When reading about the past we usually cannot tell what pressures crowded in on the person whose actions we criticize. Nor do we know what options were available to him. We must put ourselves in the place of the men and women about whom we read. What was the situation like from *their* perspective at the time? What information was available to them? Did they really have the freedom of action we assume? If we had all the intimate facts, perhaps we would find that a person we are inclined to condemn acted quite reasonably under the circumstances.

A Northerner, for example, might be tempted to blame General Robert E. Lee for resigning his commission in the United States Army and enlisting under the banner of "slavery and rebellion" in the American Civil War. But if you and I were Virginians in 1861, what would *we* have done?

The more we learn about a specific situation in history, the less we are apt to view it as an arena where the good guys on one side battle the villains on the other. (We will discuss this subject in another context in chapter eight.) Instead of studies in right versus wrong, we usually find conflicts between rival shades of gray.

The Scriptures time and again illustrate this point. Although the Hebrews of Old Testament times were uniquely chosen to be the people of God, they sometimes sank to depths of degradation worse than that of their pagan enemies. Likewise, the New Testament church was infected by charlatans, adulterers, traitors, liars and others who discredited the Christian gospel. It has been the same down through the years. Thus we who take the Bible as our guide will avoid extreme partisanship, will be discerning and sensitive in our moral judgments, and will remember that all individuals and institutions without exception are subject to the judgment of God.

Exaggerating Religious Factors
We have noted that Christians, through the reality of their own spiritual life, can enjoy an advantage in understanding the role of the spirit and, particularly, the Christian influence in history. It is simply easier to understand something that we have experienced ourselves, at least in part.

But here again we have to be careful not to exaggerate the benefits of this insight. Just as it is true that the secular-minded person may underestimate the impact of religious factors because they play such a small part in his own life, so the devout Christian may overestimate their role because they play such a profound part in his own experience. Unfortunately, many people seem to go through life with little concern for their relationship to God and little thought of eternity. Christians may find it difficult to understand a person such as King John of England (of Magna Carta fame) who seemed to be totally impervious to the claims of God or the church. (We say "seemed to be" because we really cannot know for sure what went on deep in his soul.)

Attitudes toward the Protestant Reformation are good indicators of the tendency of Christians to exaggerate the role of spiritual factors. A Roman Catholic is apt to view the Reformation solely as an impious attack on the one true Church, the bride of Christ. A Protestant, on the other hand, is apt to see it exclusively as a great spiritual movement to revive genuine New Testament Christianity. But if we study these momentous events more carefully, we find that other factors were deeply involved. Ambitious secular rulers disliked the authority held by the one great, international Church. Envious eyes scanned the landed wealth of the Church establishment. Businessmen seeking greater profits disliked Church laws restricting their freedom of action. It is true that Reformers such as Luther and Calvin were deeply religious men whose eyes were fixed squarely on the spiritual issues, but it is also true that many people lined up on either the Catholic or Protestant side for reasons that had little to do with religion. (But even when the conflict took a secular turn, spiritual factors were at stake.) It is totally unrealistic to view the Reformation as a clear-cut struggle between the good guys and the bad guys.

Their strong identification with the Bible may cause Christians to take a one-dimensional view of the role of Israel in world history. They tend to forget that the Hebrew people were just a tiny segment of the population of the ancient world, occupying only a pocket-sized bit of its land. We definitely do not want to deny their role as a people chosen of God to reveal his purposes, or their part in the story of redemption through Christ. Surely the Hebrews' contribution to world history has been far out of proportion to their numbers. But we should not make the mistake of assuming that the Old Testament is a history of the entire ancient world. It does not purport to be that. Remember that highly populated and advanced civilizations such as those of China and India are not even mentioned in the Bible.

A History of the World begun by Sir Walter Raleigh in the sixteenth century is a typical example of histories written in medieval and early modern times which display this disproportionate emphasis. He began with creation and then made the history of Israel and Judah the focal point of his description of the ancient world, with the references to Egyptians, Assyrians, Persians, Phoenicians, Greeks and other peoples built around that center. Before we criticize, we should recall that Sir Walter wrote long before modern archaeology had uncovered much of the history of the ancient peoples he dealt with so lightly. The point is, we should keep before us the fact that the Bible does not claim to be a history of the entire world of antiquity. It has other purposes. The Hebrews were of key importance in developing God's purposes for humanity, but from the standpoint of numbers, military might, power politics, certain aspects of culture and other subjects of interest to historians, they played a more modest role than some of their neighbors.

Sometimes Christians have been so anxious to find Christian heroes and heroines in history that they have claimed, as their own, men and women whose attachment to the Christian faith was very tenuous indeed. Some zealous Christians have even claimed Thomas Jefferson as their own in spite of the fact that, as a rationalist who rejected the role of the supernatural, he produced a version of the Gospels shorn of all miracles.

Christians, we conclude, do enjoy unique and valuable resources in their effort to understand the past. But we must beware of pitfalls that seem especially designed to trap unwary believers. Stumbling into them can interfere with a true understanding of the human experience and might discredit the cause of Christ.

History
and the
Christian Life   **7**

The preceding chapters have emphasized that Christians enjoy some unique advantages in understanding and appreciating the past, but at the same time face some peculiar dangers. Now let us look at the question from the opposite perspective and ask whether the study of history can in any way enrich the Christian life. Christian history professors will naturally answer with an emphatic, Yes.

Benefits to Everybody
First of all, certain general benefits from the study of history are shared by everyone who studies it.

A Sense of Identity. A knowledge of history helps each of us answer the question, Who am I? This is especially important in the face of the anonymity and alienation many people feel in our rapidly changing, mass society.

Who were my ancestors? (Bare genealogy is of little value here. I want to know what kind of people they were.) Where did they come from? When and under what circumstances did they come to my home community? What is my familial, ethnic and national heritage? What distinctive values and traits did my people represent?

One of the marks of a civilized person is a sense of his or her place between past and future. The realization that what you or I do or fail to do reflects not only on ourselves but on our family, our forefathers and our descendants should give us a greater sense of responsibility and worth. It should, for instance, cause us to be more responsible stewards of natural resources and more careful not to damage the environment we bequeath to our descendants.

The Advantage of Experience. Since history is basically the record of human experience, studying history gives us vicarious experiences that help us meet the problems of life. We learn about human nature in action, about human responses to prosperity and adversity, about the consequences of rival public and private policies.

Although historical events are unique and history never repeats itself exactly, there are enough similarities between the problems of yesterday and those of today to make experience (that is, history) a valuable tool. At the very least, a knowledge of history should help us avoid the mistakes of the past. We are told that "the only thing we learn from history is that we do not learn anything from history." If that is true, it is our own fault, not the fault of history, because the lessons are there for us to learn.

Expanding Our Sympathies. In our society we are prone to build a fence around ourselves and our little circle of family and friends and let the rest of the world go its unmerry way. This is a particularly unfortunate tendency among Christians who profess such a strong concern for the whole human race for which Christ died. History can bring us out of this narrow, self-made prison and give us opportunity to share in the lives of other people. If the people we study are very different from ourselves, so much the better.

Besides, reading history can be just plain fun. Truth is sometimes stranger than fiction, and it is always more realistic.

More Effective Citizenship. A knowledge of history helps us become more effective citizens in a democracy. If we are to vote intelligently and be a beneficial influence in our community, we must know the problems of our society, which cannot be understood apart from their historical background. Not the least of the contributions of history in this context is that a broad knowledge of the past often saves us from being taken in by pseudohistory. The more authentic history we know, the better equipped we will be to recognize misleading propaganda and other attempts to deceive.

Education for Leadership. A strong background in history is especially essential if we expect to be leaders in our communities—and Christians ought to think more seriously about their responsibilities here. Leadership implies an ability to face new and unexpected problems. Since history by its very nature is multidisciplinary, dealing with all facets of human experience, it is particularly helpful in providing the background that such responsibilities demand. And if you enter a professional field such as law, journalism, public office or the ministry, you will find a wide knowledge of past human experience a basic requirement for effective service.

Enriching Our Personalities. A knowledge of history should do something special for us as persons. It brings us into contact with all sorts of interesting people and cultures and gives us an inexhaustible fund of material for thought and conversation. It often gives us the thrill of recognition as in further reading we meet again people and ideas we have read about before.

History teaches us that life is puzzlingly complex. We find that action in one area might have unsettling effects in another, that the measures we take to solve a problem usually do not have the exact results we planned, that human beings frequently do not respond in a uniform fashion and that the big problems rarely have quick and simple answers. Knowing this ought to make us less cocksure and arrogant, more willing to listen to what other people are saying, more anxious to learn.

At the same time, history impresses us with the inevitability of change. Nothing in the human realm remains the same indefinitely. This ought on the one hand to make us more philosophical in the face of adversity, remembering that "this, too, will pass." On the other hand it should encourage us to cling to the eternal values that do not change.

Special Benefits to Christians

In addition to these more general benefits, history can contribute specifically and substantially to Christian understanding and growth.

What God Is Like. Perhaps you learned in church school or confirmation class that God is omnipotent, omniscient, omnipresent, changeless and all-loving. But did you ever stop to think that these attributes of God would be for us only abstractions if we knew nothing about how he has actually dealt with human beings in history?

The Scriptures do not limit themselves to expressing abstract ideas concerning the nature of God. Concrete and vivid narratives of his acts on the human scene show him to be powerful, just and loving. In particular, the nature of God is revealed through his Son, who came into the world and participated in historical events as recorded in the Gospels by eyewitnesses.

Christ in action—healing the sick, throwing the money-changers out of the Temple, sharing the good news with his followers on hillsides or seashores and (most importantly) dying on the cross and then appearing to his disciples after his resurrection—impresses on our minds the attributes of God more forcefully than could any abstract definition. And in the two thousand years since New Testament times, he has continued to reveal himself as powerful, just and loving in the experiences of those who put their trust in him. That is, he is revealed in the personal histories of his people.

A Better Understanding of the Bible. A knowledge of history also increases our understanding of the Bible itself. The more we know about the history of the ancient Near East and Mediterranean areas—especially the customs, beliefs and practices of the people—the better we will understand the teachings of Scripture. There are many nuances that we completely miss if we do not know the milieu in which the biblical events took place.

It is impossible, for example, to understand the dilemma of the Jewish people and the embryonic Christian church in New Testament times without some basic knowledge of the Roman Empire and its policies toward subject peoples and religious groups. What was the position of the Herods? of Pontius Pilate? of the publicans? of the centurions? What kind of men were the Caesars—Augustus, Tiberius, Nero? What was implied by the Roman citizenship Paul enjoyed? Why was the persecution of the early Christians so erratic? What special conditions facilitated the rapid spread of Christianity in the first century?

Such examples can be multiplied a hundredfold and more. We are not suggesting that the story of redemption does not shine through the Scriptures without such background information. But certainly important implications of the Bible narrative remain hidden unless we are acquainted with the world in which these events took place.

Clarification of Christian Doctrine. Through a study of church history we can see how key Christian doctrines have been clarified since the apostolic period. In the first centuries of the Christian era, for example, there was considerable confusion about the divine-human nature of Christ. A group now called the Arians claimed that he was a created being and thus inferior to the Father. After a furious controversy lasting for decades, the Council of Nicaea (A.D. 325) framed a statement affirming that Jesus Christ is "of one substance with the Father," a central tenet of the Christian faith. This doctrine is contained in the Scriptures to be sure, but it took a long historical struggle to clear up some serious misconceptions concerning it.

History can shed light on other spiritual issues as well. Should Christians withdraw physically from the world to develop their inward spiritual resources in places of refuge far from the sin and secular preoccupations of the world? Or should we risk contamination by these temptations in order to minister in the busy marketplace? The pros and cons of this issue were lived out in real-life situations that we read about especially in the history of the Middle Ages.

The crucial Christian doctrine of salvation by faith alone, obscured for centuries by a multitude of "works," was proclaimed from the housetops by Martin Luther and other Reformers. To learn the implications of this basic doctrine, we can do no better than study the heated events, debates, pamphlets and treatises of this critical period of history.

Should church services be liturgical, dignified and stately, or simple, informal and animated? Should Christians hold public office, serve in the military or involve themselves in campaigns for social reform? By studying the history of groups of Christians on both sides of such questions, we will see amply illustrated not only the arguments of all sides but their consequences in the actual experiences of Christian people. There is hardly a single issue confronting the Christian that cannot be illuminated by a study of the history of the Christian community down through the years.

Vindicating the Bible's View of Human Nature.   Many people ask (and Christians should too) whether the truths of Scripture correspond to reality. For example, is the Bible's picture of humanity—inclined to evil but redeemable—correct? Are human beings in fact capable of both the foulest crimes and the noblest deeds, as the Bible portrays? Have people's lives really been transformed through a new birth such as is described by Christ (Jn. 3:3-15)? Do people really live and act as the characters in the Bible narratives did— sometimes obedient, sometimes not—or does the Bible present a false, contrived picture of human personality?

An essential element of the Christian faith is a commitment to the standard of personal and public morality as set forth in the Scriptures. This commitment implies a conviction that God established this standard to promote human well-being and that violating it produces failure and distress. Has human experience as recorded in history authenticated this biblical blueprint for human happiness?

As you study history and think about people's deeds and misdeeds, you will find it exciting to ask such questions and learn the extent to which history validates the Bible's teachings.

A Prerequisite for Christian Service.   It is probably unnecessary to stress the fact that a knowledge of history is a prerequisite for many kinds of Christian service. Note the number of historical references your pastor uses to illustrate sermons. Effective ministry obviously requires a knowledge of the historical background of the country or area of service. If Christians are to have any useful impact on the world, we will naturally have to know enough about the background of the people we endeavor to serve to understand and appreciate their customs and outlook.

At the very least, such basic knowledge will help prevent blunders that offend or wound those whose confidence we are trying to gain. History is not the only subject that serves this purpose, but it is one of the most important.

Claims of the Cults. Traditional cults are growing, and new ones seem to arise every day. Many of these cults, old and new, are built around heresies which Christians long ago faced and rejected. A sound knowledge of history will provide the ammunition often needed to puncture false claims, particularly those parading under the banner of Christianity. For instance, Christian Science and Theosophy both include features of the gnostic sect with which Christianity had to deal in its early centuries. The current Children of God (COG) sect carries overtones of antinomianism with its claim that Christians are not obligated to obey the moral law. In common with earlier heresies, the Unification Church of Reverend Sun Myung Moon denies the deity of Christ and the substitutionary nature of his death. Our response to these current challenges can be more balanced and mature if we learn from history the way earlier Christians handled very similar threats.

Interpreting Prophecy. Authentic historical knowledge will help us evaluate various interpretations of biblical prophecy. It will assist us in showing how prophecies were fulfilled in the past through concrete historical events. And since prophecies concerning events still in the future involve historical events which are to transpire before their fulfillment, history will help the conscientious Bible student determine whether the time is ripe for such fulfillment.

A strong word of caution is required here, however. Far too many *conjectures* have been presented as *fact*. The passing years have discredited a long list of overconfident predictions. Many of these have been based on faulty historical knowledge. The more we know about history, the more cautious we are apt to be in stating how a specific occurrence fits into the pattern of biblical prophecy.

When I was a teenager, "experts" in the field of prophecy confidently claimed that recent and current historical events all pointed to Benito Mussolini as the antichrist, since he was the ruler of a "revived Roman Empire." That kind of false prediction soured many members of my generation on the whole subject of biblical prophecy—a regrettable misfortune. The "experts' " heavy reliance on conjecture has caused many reputable Christian historians to be very wary (perhaps too wary) of the whole field of biblical prophecy.

The Inspiration of Heroic Christians. History can also provide the encouragement and inspiration needed in the Christian life. On its pages we find that other people have endured the same disappointments and suffering that we face and worse, and have found God true to his promises. We can profit from the ways others have dealt with specific problems surprisingly similar to our own. Remember that biography, properly written, is one of the most useful forms of history. It gets down to the nitty-gritty of human experience.

You will not find that faithfulness to God and his standards has always brought fame and fortune. You will find that sometimes it has brought frustration and sorrow rather than what the world calls success. But this too vindicates the Scripture's picture of human experience. Do you recall what finally happened to New Testament greats such as Stephen and James and Paul? We do not need to glamorize the lives of Christian heroes and heroines, as some biographers have mistakenly done, to make them appear "successful" and "fulfilled" in human terms. It is obvious that God's definition of success is not the same as that of the world.

Let History Judge. Have you ever observed how often unworthy people seem to "flourish as the green bay tree" while selfless and dedicated men and women labor and sacrifice and suffer to serve the underprivileged and advance the kingdom of God and receive little or no recognition for their labors? How many faithful missionaries, linguists and Bible translators have toiled to bring the gospel to the pagan world, and have hardly been noticed? Here the Christian historian and biographer have a great opportunity to rectify the injustice inherent in such omissions, broaden the scope of our understanding of the past and inspire us with examples of Christian faith in action.

Credit Where Credit Was Due.   In his palace at Shushan, Persia's King Ahasuerus tossed and turned on his royal bed, but sleep just would not come. Desperate, he finally commanded a chamberlain to bring in the historical chronicles of his reign. As these were read to him, he learned that two members of his palace guard some time previously had conspired to assassinate him, but were thwarted by the vigilance of an elderly Jew named Mordecai.

"What honor or dignity has been bestowed on Mordecai for this?" the king demanded.

"Nothing has been done for him."

Whereupon, the king, to correct this grave injustice, arranged to have Mordecai arrayed in the king's robe and crown, mounted on the royal charger and paraded through the streets of the capital as a "man whom the king delights to honor" (Esther 6:1-11).

The record does not tell us why in his sleeplessness the king ordered the historical records read to him. Did he value the study of history and wish to put these wakeful hours to good use? Or did he consider reading history the perfect cure for insomnia, as so many of your fellow students do?

At any rate, we know that King Ahasuerus used his new knowledge of history to give credit where credit was due and to rectify a wrong. Whether you become a professional historian or remain an interested amateur, the study of history can help you, like Ahasuerus, not only to gain a better understanding of the past but to perform more effectively in the present.

When Christians Look Back

8

In chapter one we mentioned that the Christian has two concepts of history: the typical classroom approach, dealing with more or less concrete human events and movements here on earth, and "redemption (or salvation) history," dealing with God's grand strategy for the salvation of mankind. For nearly two thousand years Christians have proclaimed the second of these to the world as the core of the gospel, the good news.

This is the message that has inspired Christians down through the centuries to face suffering and martyrdom, as well as the toils and pains of ordinary life. We must emphasize again that this message concerning God's eternal purposes for humanity is not the product of historical research and documentation; it is not amenable to this kind of evidence. The Christian believes that the gospel comes to us through divine revelation. Friend and foe alike agree that it is accepted—if it is accepted at all—by faith.

Convictions about the Fall and God's strategy for redeeming the human race form the basis of the Christian's whole outlook on the human personality, the world and all the events of history. For this reason it is both difficult and undesirable to separate in the Christian's mind the two views of history we are discussing.

This final chapter asks some fundamental questions about the Christian view of the past, not in order to present eighteen-carat, authoritative answers on a silver platter (no one is capable of doing that), but to alert you to certain issues and to encourage further study and thought.

Is the history usually taught in the classroom a purely secular affair? Can we agree with a certain Christian philosopher's claim that since Satan is the ruler of this world Christians need not relate their faith to the study of "secular" history?[1] Are not all the men, women, boys and girls who figure in classroom history human beings for whom Christ died and the objects of his concern? In chapter seven we showed that even "secular" history helps us understand our Christian faith better. Christians will assuredly be appalled and grieved by the enormity of human debasement as revealed in history. But just as surely God's Spirit has been at work in human affairs through the centuries.

As you endeavor to apply the world view inherent in "redemption history" to the subject matter of your history courses in school, you will come face to face with some extremely thorny issues that should now engage our attention.

The Kingdom Is in the Midst of You
In the first place, the expectation of Christ's second coming and the establishment of his glorious future kingdom—just because it is the very essence of the Christian hope and the event toward which all history is moving—unfortunately

may cause us to focus our eyes so exclusively on a future event that we forget we can fulfill God's purposes right here and now. Remember that the New Testament phrase *kingdom of God* refers not only to this longed-for future consummation when Jesus Christ is crowned King of kings and Lord of lords, but also to his rule—in the past and right now—over all those who accept him in faith.

We are inclined to draw charts and diagrams showing "God's Eternal Plan of Redemption" and forget that the "plan" is only a cold abstraction. We must be reminded that it is people, real flesh-and-blood human beings, for whom Christ died and for whom he is coming again. God's purpose in history is the development of sons and daughters who conform to the image of Christ. And every person who has ever lived is important for his or her own sake and is of equal value in God's sight. Christ Jesus derives just as much pleasure from a life lived for his glory in ancient Bithynia or medieval Bohemia as from those who greet him with uplifted hands at his second coming.

To use the illustration of Sir Herbert Butterfield, an outstanding Christian historian of England, "History is not like a train, the sole purpose of which is to get to its destination." It is more like a Beethoven symphony. "The point of it is not saved up until the end, the whole of it is not a mere preparation for a beauty that is only to be achieved in the last bar."[2] We can enjoy God's beauty and love today as well as on that great tomorrow toward which all history is moving.

This truth can also be a corrective to ordinary classroom history. Since historians by the very nature of their craft must concentrate on the comparatively few people who contribute conspicuously to change, we need to remind ourselves that all people everywhere are the object of God's concern and are featured in *his* history book, regardless of whether they had anything to do with some pivotal event we thought worthy of recording.

The Hidden Conflict

Another feature of the Christian view of the past that may involve perplexities is the conviction that history reflects an age-old and constant struggle between good and evil, between God and Satan. That such a struggle is a reality is the distinct teaching of the Scriptures from Genesis to Revelation. The problem is that rarely does this struggle, at least on the surface, involve a clear-cut conflict between what is totally right and totally wrong or between shining saints and grubby sinners.

We are tempted to become a bit cynical because propagandists for the rival sides of an issue so frequently hide selfish motives behind a smokescreen of lofty ideals. We need to be on our guard against being misled by such trickery. Christian students must balance themselves on the thin line between skepticism on the one hand and failure to recognize the very real conflict in the world between good and evil on the other.

Sometimes, of course, it is not so very difficult to identify the right with one side or the other. In some cases, for example when people are defending themselves against a cruel aggressor or when a persecuted minority is struggling for liberty, the preponderance of right is clear. But the simple fact that a group of people is struggling for the right does not necessarily imply that they are people of unalloyed virtue. During World War 2 the Christian men in my U.S. Eighth Air Force unit were often pained by the immorality, drunkenness and foul language of their non-Christian comrades. But they could still believe that the Nazi tyranny was so thoroughly debased that the conflict in which they were engaged could legitimately be regarded as a struggle between good and evil.

In other words, it is necessary to distinguish between the people involved in a conflict and the principles at issue. The situation really becomes sticky when we find ungodly people supporting right causes (perhaps for the wrong reasons) and godly people forced by circumstances or misapprehensions to support wrong ones. Can you imagine the tragically ambivalent situation faced by Christian youth drafted into the army of Nazi Germany?

Most historians recognize a conflict in the world between good and evil. At least they tend to condemn evil in its most blatant, outward manifestations. They are much less likely to recognize the sources of evil acts—wrong beliefs, spiritual waywardness and the activity of Satan. They probably would not share the Christian's conviction that expansion of Christ's rule in the hearts of men and women is the clearest manifestation of victory of good over evil.

The book that was for centuries the most influential literary and historical work in the Western world—St. Augustine's *City of God*—made this conflict the key to all history. World history to him was the scene of a perpetual conflict between two "cities"—the City of Earth, composed of all those who seek reward and happiness on earth, and the City of God, composed of all those who faithfully give their allegiance to the heavenly kingdom. Note that St. Augustine did not identify the two cities with the Roman state and the Christian church, respectively. The cities are symbols of two spiritual powers that have always contended for the allegiance of God's creation.

What side is God on? He is always on the side of right, of course. But what side is that?

The Bible contains innumerable divine promises to strengthen and prosper the people who serve God and keep his commandments. But it also contains many instances of divine judgment. Time and time again pagan nations were the instruments of that judgment as God punished his chosen people for their infidelity and moral delinquencies. For instance, God commissioned the heathen and impious Chaldeans to invade Judah, destroy Jerusalem, and drag the Jews as captives to Babylon. This does not imply that the Chaldeans were saintly heroes; far from it. In this instance, as in many others, God used an evil, tyrannical power to accomplish his judgment. Whose side then should we say God was on?

Such considerations should discourage us from oversimplifying the struggle between good and evil in the world. Remember that God sees much more than we do and thus his ways often seem mysterious and inexplicable to us.

"His" Story or Man's Story?

By all odds the most complex historical issue—and the issue on which Christians have taken the most vehement and contradictory stands—is the question of how much control God exercises over human decisions and the events of history. This issue is the most profound one because it affects not only our outlook on both past and present but our whole attitude toward God himself and his dealings with us. The issue is so basic, and so difficult to compromise, that it has divided Christians into opposing camps, split church congregations and denominations, and, as you have probably noticed already, inspired the loudest, most vociferous college bull sessions. Any position we take on the issue immediately provokes spirited objections. The books written on it could easily fill a college library. The most we can do here is briefly summarize what the debate is about.

Scores of different positions have been taken on the issue of the role of God in history. These can generally be grouped under three main headings: (1) God exercises no control or, at least, he is left out of the discussion, which may amount to about the same thing; (2) God exercises complete control—he has actively willed everything that has happened; (3) God is in ultimate control and intervenes in history, but has left considerable room for exercise of the human will. In other words, history can be said to be made by man alone, by God alone or by God and man.

By Man Alone. Some authors (notably writers, such as Karl Marx, who do not recognize that God even exists) categorically deny that God plays any part in history. More likely, however, the historian is apt just to leave God out of the discussion. Many, probably the majority, describe and analyze events and movements without any mention of ultimate causation.

Of those who discuss causation, some claim that geographic environment is the controlling factor; others point to economics; still others, to internal human drives such as "the will to power." Some historians have contended that history has its own laws of development, such as the law of progress that we discussed in chapter four. Eighteenth-century deists believed that before the dawn of time God established certain natural laws to govern the universe and then abdicated immediate control.

Even dedicated Christian historians can easily discuss a segment of the past without reference to God's part in it, probably because it is not at all apparent what that part was and it would be presumptuous to speculate. Just what *was* God's role, for example, in the Jay Treaty or the 1849 California Gold Rush or the building of the Suez Canal?

But to assume that human beings by themselves have determined the course of history is an untenable position. Of course, it is common to discuss the role of human decision in individual historical events. The Pilgrims decided to found a colony in the American wilderness; Napoleon Bonaparte decided to invade Russia. But who could anticipate the long-term effects of these or any other human decisions? When Martin Luther decided to post his Ninety-five Theses on the church door at Wittenberg, could he have anticipated the upheaval of European society that would result? When Orville and Wilbur Wright managed to get their primitive flying contraption airborne on that famous day at Kitty Hawk in 1903, were they planning to revolutionize not only transportation but also warfare and the whole international scene?

It is a commonplace among historians that major long-range movements of history were not the consequence of deliberate human planning or decision. No man or woman or group of people sat down and decided that there was to be an industrial revolution or a westward movement across America or an expansion of European culture around the world. Historians may conclude that history is chaos, that it is ruled by mere chance or moves according to its own internal dynamic, but not that it has been made by deliberate human decision or planning.

By God Alone. Nothing could be more natural and consistent than for a Christian to believe that God intervenes in human history. God is not some vague, ethereal being floating around beyond the farthest star who has left his people to struggle on alone in a universe of chance or chaos. The Scriptures over and over declare, and the experience of unnumbered Christians confirms, that God is here and he is at work. Are we not instructed to pray for guidance and for divine help in troubles great and small? And have we not ourselves seen such prayers answered—affirmatively?

Obviously, for the Christian the question is not, Does God intervene in human history? The question rather concerns the nature of that intervention and whether or not by the exercise of free will man can counteract God's purposes.

The doctrine that God is in complete, exclusive control of everything that happens in history—that it is *his* story—was introduced into the thinking of the church largely by St. Augustine, bishop of Hippo, in the fifth century. He developed the doctrine in reaction to the Pelagian heresy, which held that the human will is the determining factor in the salvation of the individual.

St. Augustine's position is essentially quite simple. It is based on the total, absolute sovereignty of God. Everything, without exception (whether good, bad or indifferent), that has ever happened has occurred in accordance with God's will. It is impossible for man or woman to counter that will. Even when we appear to be disobeying God's ordinance, we are actually furthering his plan because God uses the disobedience to accomplish his purposes. Nothing happens by chance; nothing happens by independent human agency. In the words of St. Augustine:

> Nothing, therefore, happens unless the Omnipotent wills it to happen. He either allows it to happen or he actually causes it to happen....
>
> Unless we believe this, the very beginning of our Confession of Faith is imperiled—the sentence in which we profess to believe in God the Father Almighty. For he is called Almighty for no other reason than that he can do whatsoever he willeth and because the efficacy of his omnipotent will is not impeded by the will of any creature....
>
> In a strange and ineffable fashion even that which is done against his will is not done without his will. For it would not be done without his allowing it—and surely his permission is not unwilling but willing.[3]

St. Augustine and his followers claim that before time began, God, for reasons beyond the understanding of finite man, willed not only the plan of redemption but also all the apparently tragic events that have occurred in human history. To believe otherwise is to hold that the universe is not really under God's control.

Those who hold this position stress the power and glorious greatness of God and are very sensitive to any affront to his sovereign majesty. They assert that granting human beings the power to act against God's will denies the absolute sovereignty of God. If we can disobey God's will, then his power is not absolute.

They further emphasize that dependence on the absolute

sovereignty of God is a source of confidence and comfort to Christian believers, since nothing can happen in life that their heavenly Father has not ordained.

Naturally the Augustinian position has been subjected to intense criticism from Christians holding contrary views regarding the role of the human will. They claim that St. Augustine misinterpreted the Scriptures he quoted. They allege that the doctrine makes human beings puppets rather than free individuals created in the image of God. By robbing human beings of the power of choice, it relieves them of responsibility for their actions. Critics also claim that the doctrine makes God the cause of all the injustice and misery since the world began. By making evil a part of God's plan, the critics state that it erases the distinction between right and wrong and makes the age-old conflict between God and Satan a sham.

To this criticism the defenders of God's absolute sovereignty reply that "now we see through a glass darkly." Because God's ways and motives are hid, they ask, are they therefore unjust?

By God and Man. Christians who hold this third view obviously give human beings a more important role in determining the course of history, although they differ appreciably about the extent of that role. Some come fairly close to the Augustinian position, others differ radically from it.

In general, the proponents of this third view maintain that our ability and responsibility to choose—especially between right and wrong—is what gives us our stature as children of God. They point out that the Bible everywhere calls on men and women to choose, to turn, to exercise their will in accepting or rejecting the salvation God offers.

At the same time, these Christians must discover some sort of accommodation between this human free will and God's sovereignty. God must have given up some of his sovereignty (at least temporarily) when he gave human beings the power to choose between good and evil. God has purposed nothing but good from the Garden of Eden on, but people have used this freedom to choose their own will rather than God's, thus bringing misery, sorrow and death into the world. The conflict between God and Satan is real and the human will is the battleground.

On the other hand, those who hold this third view maintain that history is also not made by man alone. God intervenes. He guides, supports, admonishes and punishes. Sir Herbert Butterfield illustrated his view of the relationship between God's sovereignty and man's will with the analogy of God as a great composer and his children as mistake-prone members of the orchestra:

> We must imagine that the composer himself is only composing the music inch by inch as the orchestra is playing it; so that if you and I play wrong notes he changes his mind and gives a different turn to the bars that come immediately afterwards, as though saying to himself: "We can only straighten out this piece of untidiness if we pass for a moment from the major into the minor key." Indeed the composer of the piece leaves himself room for great elasticity, until we ourselves have shown what we are going to do next; although when the music has actually been played over and had become a thing of the past we may be tempted to imagine that it is just as he had intended it to be all the time—that the whole course of things had been inevitable from the first.[5]

In this view, human beings by their sin and folly can counter God's will, but only at great risk since God's patience will not last forever. Moreover, God is not thwarted, because he can turn human rebellion to his own purposes. Romans 8:28 says, "In everything God works for good with those who love him." This passage does not imply that "everything" was decreed by God, but that whatever people have done can be used by God for the good of his children.

Why is there so much evil and suffering in the world? Because man has misused the free will God has given him. Why, then, does not God withdraw that gift and compel us to do the right? Because then we would be mere machines or beasts ruled by instinct, rather than human beings who can freely love and praise God.

The critics of this position claim that it is totally unscriptural in limiting the majesty and omnipotence of God, that it interprets God too much in human terms, that it does not explain why God controls events at certain times and not at others, and that it puts human history too much at the mercy of finite men and women. They emphasize that salvation is the work of God and God alone; to assert that the human will plans a part in that salvation is to downgrade God's grace in Christ.

We may never be able to solve this question of the role of divine sovereignty and human will in history. But you are encouraged to research the problem on your own and come to your own conclusions. Think through each position and ask yourself relevant questions. How much of a free agent am I? Could I really have decided and acted in a different way than I did? Or did God ordain from the foundation of the universe that I would make the decision I did? Depending on how you answer these questions, you may decide that St. Augustine or Sir Herbert Butterfield was right or that there is some other solution to this perplexity.

This brief summary does not do justice to the various ways of looking at the question of God's control over history. It should alert you, however, to the general nature of the controversy and whet your appetite to learn more.

What History Does Not Tell
While the heated debate among these schools of thought continues, the protagonists can agree on one point: history

itself is of little help in arriving at an answer. The events of history themselves do not show whether or not God ordained them. You or I could spend a lifetime studying the establishment of the Jamestown colony and become the world's foremost authority on the subject, but all our research would be of little assistance in determining whether or not God ordained that settlement. The conviction that God did, or did not, control the actions of the participants is a religious conviction not susceptible to historical research. The historian does not have the tools to settle such questions. As we study history it is important that we recognize its limitations.

The Hand of God.   Specific incidents of alleged divine intervention in history have inspired many intriguing debates among historians. To some extent these incidents and debates illustrate the inherent limitations of history. During the "Dark Age of Latin Learning," men and women saw the immediate hand of God or the intervention of the saints in all kinds of affairs, both great and small. A slight case of the sniffles was a sign of God's displeasure. A flight of birds overhead or a sudden breeze had divine significance. The "Golden Legend" pictured the saints as living amid almost daily miracles and moving freely between the seen and the unseen worlds. We must ask ourselves two questions here: Did the alleged miracles actually occur? Does every event somehow reflect the immediate hand of God?

In A.D. 312 a pagan commander, Constantine, was leading his troops against rivals competing for the Roman imperial throne. Suddenly Constantine saw in the sky overhead a vision of a flaming cross, brighter than the noonday sun, with the inscription *In hoc signo vinces* ("In this sign thou shalt conquer"). Constantine had the chi-rho emblem of Christ emblazoned on the shields of his troops, won the Battle of the Milvian Bridge and eventually became the first Christian emperor. (There are a number of variations of this story.)

In fifteenth-century France a seventeen-year-old peasant girl, Joan of Arc, heard mysterious voices directing her to rescue her country from its English enemies. She responded, was accepted as commander of the French armies and turned the tide of the Hundred Years' War.

In 1588, Spain, at the zenith of her power, launched her Invincible Armada in a projected invasion of England. If successful, Spain could have forced England back into the Catholic fold. The great expedition was frustrated not only by the English navy but by a violent so-called Protestant storm which arose at just the right moment.

In 1944, certain specific weather conditions were absolutely required to make the Allies' D-Day landings successful. After many days of unfavorable weather, on the appointed day the conditions were right.

Did these events occur as described? If so, did they reflect God's immediate intervention in human affairs? The first question lends itself to historical investigation and thus involves a legitimate use of the historian's craft. But the second is not the kind of question that a historian—as a historian—can answer. Was the storm that discomfited the Spanish Armada sent by God? We know from solid historical evidence that the storm did occur, but there was nothing in the wind itself to tell us whether or not God had sent it. To believe that it reflected God's intervention is an act of religious faith. To reject that belief, or any such belief, is also an act of religious faith. Our attitude toward such questions reflects the basic presuppositions which we bring to our study of the human past.

Complexities. This subject of God's hand in history is far more complex than it first appears. Note, for instance, that in each of the famous incidents we have mentioned, God is pictured as intervening miraculously on the side of the right (although everyone will not agree which side was right). It is certainly consistent with the Christian's faith to believe that he intervened. But why did not similar miracles occur to thwart "the enemy" on various other occasions; when, for example, the Moslems finally stormed Constantinople in 1453 or the Bolsheviks grasped control of Russia in 1917? Why did not God act to protect the Jews against Hitler's holocaust during World War 2?

Further, is the hand of God to be seen only in apparent miracles which seem to advance "God's cause" in the world? (Who decides what "God's cause" is and what will advance it?) Or does God also act in what appear to be purely mundane matters? Did he also send the storms that protected thirteenth-century pagan Japan from invasion by the pagan Mongols? Is God's hand at work in the world all the time or only on special occasions?

The Miracle Within. A discussion of miracles is also relevant to this question of the limits of historical inquiry. There are different categories of miracles. An *absolute miracle* could only be a miracle and nothing else (Christ raising Lazarus from the dead). A *providential miracle* involves a natural phenomenon that occurs at a most opportune time (say, for example, the weather in the English Channel in 1944). Some might call it a mere coincidence.

A third category is so common among Christians that they may not even recognize it as a miracle at all—God working directly in the *human heart*. Here, again, the evidences are not susceptible to the usual kinds of historical investigation. We cannot prove by any kind of documentation that it was God who sent St. Augustine of Canterbury to the pagan Anglo-Saxons in 597, or inspired Christopher Columbus to embark on his fateful voyage in 1492, or gave Abraham Lincoln inner strength in the darkest days of the Civil War. But does that prove that he did not?

We know God works in history because he works in our own hearts. A divine miracle gave us new life in Christ. It is God who helps us overcome temptation, gives us strength in adversity, replaces hatred with love and fear of tomorrow with hope of a share in his everlasting kingdom.

Making History

We have come full circle and are back to the concept of history as human experience, a theme we introduced in chapter two. History embraces the entire past experience of the human race. Just as our own individual lives take on more significance and purpose when we examine our personal experiences, so the world around us takes on new significance as we study the experiences of society at large.

Remember that a working definition of the term "history" as a field of knowledge involves an *explanation* of past events, not merely a recital of what happened. Since history is not a study of the past itself but of the record of the past, and since that record is often erroneous, biased, incomplete or embarrassingly voluminous, just the task of learning what happened can require an engrossing bit of detective work. But then having learned what actually occurred, we must ask ourselves why it happened, what issues were involved and what consequences ensued. It is this effort to analyze and explain that makes history a challenging and absorbing enterprise.

Historians come up with contrasting answers to the questions we have raised because they bring different presuppositions and values to their inquiries. Christians look at the past in a distinctive way because they bring to their study of the human experience a distinctive Christian frame of reference and system of values. The validity of this Christian view of the past rests directly on the validity of the Christian faith itself.

As a Christian student, you face the task of integrating your faith with secular learning to form a comprehensive and consistent world view. Just as we evaluate our individual experiences in the light of our convictions about God and his purposes for our lives, so we must endeavor to relate the specific and concrete events of history learned through scholarly investigation ("classroom history") to the truths concerning God's strategy for human redemption accepted by faith ("redemption history").

In the case of both, the key factor is the individual human being, created in the image of God with inestimable worth, fallen but redeemable. It was for all human beings that Jesus Christ entered history, died and rose again. It is this infinite human worth that gives significance to so-called mundane history and raises our studies above a mechanical narrative of events long past.

Bibliographical Notes

To learn more about the relationship between Christian faith and history, the place to begin is, of course, the Scriptures themselves. The main purpose should not be to locate isolated verses or passages that touch on this relationship (although their importance should not be discounted), but to note how, in a broad context, the Bible develops its historical narrative and how history is involved in its fundamental teachings.

Before proceeding any further, you might read Kenneth Scott Latourette's address, "The Christian Understanding of History," in the *American Historical Review*, LIV (1949), 259-67. Latourette, an evangelical Christian, reached the top of the historians' profession in the United States when in 1948 he became president of the American Historical Association. In this inaugural address he stated clearly and unequivocally the Christian foundations of his view of history. He emphasized that "a Christian's belief about what happens beyond history is what gives relevance to his research on what happens inside it."

A comprehensive history of historical writing from ancient times to the present based on evangelical faith and values is not available and its preparation remains a challenge to the community of Christian scholars. As an introduction to historical writing, however, you could consult Page Smith's *The Historian and History* (New York: Alfred A. Knopf, 1964). *Christianity and History* (Princeton, N.J. Princeton

Univ. Press, 1964), a collection of essays by Princeton scholar E. Harris Harbison, is impressive, as it uncovers the many-sided relationships between Christian faith and history. See especially his chapters on religious perspectives on college teaching of history and on John Calvin's view of history.

In 1948 Sir Herbert Butterfield, in a series of lectures to Cambridge University students, described not only his own strong convictions about the ways his Christian faith related to the study of history but also the stance he believed the Christian historian should take in interpreting the past. You will find these lectures in a thin volume also entitled *Christianity and History* (New York: Scribner, 1949, 1950). He developed his perspectives further in *History and Human Relations* (London: Collins, 1951). Note here especially his treatment of Marxist history.

Roman Catholics with their own long institutional history have a strong interest in the relationship between faith and history. Evangelical students will respond particularly to the works of Christopher Dawson, who makes the forthright claim that religion is the key to history. See his *Dynamics of World History* (London: Sheed and Ward, 1956).

C. T. McIntire brings together twenty-three essays by twenty-two prominent historians, theologians and other writers in *God, History, and Historians* (New York: Oxford Univ. Press, 1977). Since almost all of these essays were written since World War 2 they give the reader an excellent picture of the variety of thinking on the subject during the past generation.

A Christian View of History?, edited by George Marsden and Frank Roberts (Grand Rapids, Mich.: Eerdmans, 1975) contains articles by nine Christian historians (six teaching at Calvin College) which provide samples of various Christian approaches to historical scholarship. Be sure to read M. Howard Rienstra's bibliographical essay at the close of the book. Dr. Rienstra divides his essay into sections on Christianity and history for historians, philosophers and theologians. The first section is especially recommended as a guide for further study by history students.

The Conference on Faith and History is an organization of evangelical historians in the United States. Its periodical *Fides et Historia* contains many articles and book reviews helpful to students seeking to integrate their faith with their study of history and to keep up with the latest developments in the field.

Notes

Chapter 1

[1]*Webster's New Collegiate Dictionary* (Springfield, Mass.: G. and C. Merriam Co., 1975), p. 543.

Chapter 2

[1]William L. Shirer, *The Rise and Fall of the Third Reich* (Greenwich, Conn.: Fawcett Pub., 1962), p. xii.

[2]From an unpublished professional evaluation.

[3]This is an excerpt from a student's paper. Probably the Christian student's most effective response to hostility to his faith on the part of an instructor is simply to find occasion to identify himself as a Christian. This may open the door of opportunity to present to the class a Christian position.

Chapter 3

[1]George Rawlinson, Richard Crawley and R. Feelham, trans., *The History of Herodotus and the History of the Peloponnesian War by Thucydides*, Great Books of the Western World, VI (Chicago: Encyclopedia Britannica, 1952), p. 1.

[2]Ibid., p. 354.

Chapter 4

[1]Arnold Joseph Toynbee, *A Study of History*, I-XII (New York: Oxford Univ. Press, 1935-61).

[2]Henry Wadsworth Longfellow quoted in Tryon Edwards, ed., *The New Dictionary of Thoughts*, rev. Ralph Emerson Browns et al. (Standard Book Company, 1964), p. 272.

[3]Toynbee, XII.

[4]Thomas Carlyle, *On Heroes, Hero-Worship, and the Heroic in History* (Boston: Houghton Mifflin, 1907), p. 18.

[5]Ibid.

[6]Auguste Comte, *The Positive Philosophy*, trans. and rev. Harriet Martineau (Chicago: Belford, Clarke & Co., 1853).

[7]Marx and Engels were prolific writers. For a brief summary of their doctrines written in forceful language for propaganda purposes, see *The Communist Manifesto*, ed. D. Ryazanoff (New York: Russell & Russell, 1963).

[8]Shirer, p. 333.

Chapter 5

[1]Several Scripture passages refer to man's being created in the image (or likeness) of God. See especially Gen. 1:26. We can understand this to mean that we are spiritual beings capable of immortality; that we are rational and morally responsible beings related to God as are no other creatures on earth. Even after the Fall man is referred to in the Scriptures as created in God's image (Gen. 9:6; Jas. 3:9). But his fallen nature is in need of being "renewed in knowledge after the image of its creator" (Col. 3:10). For a discussion of the term *image*, see Derek Kidner, *Genesis* (Downers Grove, Ill.: InterVarsity Press, 1967), pp. 50-51.

[2]Charles R. Erdman, *The Gospel of Matthew* (Philadelphia: Westminster Press, 1948), pp. 58-59.

[3]The term *value* is closely related to, but not quite the same as, the term *perspective* used in chapter two. Our perspective is the vantage point from which we view the past and is more or less intrinsic to our position in life. Our system of values, on the other hand, is the standard by which we judge people, movements and ideas, and is consciously or subconsciously chosen by each individual.

[4]John M. Good, *The Shaping of Western Society* (New York: Holt, Rinehart and Winston, 1968), p. 43. The paragraph quoted is followed by some of the moral teachings of Jesus selected from the Sermon on the Mount. This text is not criticized here for failing to accept Christian doctrines as true. It is criticized for failing to state what Christians hold to be true.

[5]R. R. Palmer and Joel Colton, *A History of the Modern World*, 5th ed. (New York: Alfred A. Knopf, 1978), p. 304.

[6]Sydney E. Ahlstrom, *A Religious History of the American People* (New Haven, Conn.: Yale Univ. Press, 1972), p. 8.

[7]*A History of the Expansion of Christianity*, VI (New York: Harper and Brothers, 1944).

Chapter 6

[1]Konrad Heiden, *Der Fuehrer* (Boston: Houghton Mifflin, 1944). Chapter one is particularly applicable.

[2]Ahlstrom, pp. 8, 733-34, 798-99, 849-50. See also Josiah Strong, *Our Country* (Cambridge: Harvard Univ., Belknap Press, 1963).

Chapter 8

[1]Karl Löwith, *Meaning in History* (Chicago: Univ. of Chicago Press, 1955). This philosopher represents positions on basic issues involving history as a field of study which are diametrically opposed to some of those taken in the present discussion. For example, in his "Conclusion" (pp. 191-203), he states: "Historical processes as such do not bear the least evidence of a comprehensive and ultimate meaning.... The importance of secular history decreases in direct proportion to the intensity of man's concern with God and himself.... Christians are not a historical people." Löwith displays a wide knowledge of history, however, and that knowledge appears to have been very useful to him in reaching his conclusions.

[2]Herbert Butterfield, *Christianity and History* (New York: Scribner, 1949, 1950), p. 67.

[3]Albert C. Outler, ed. *Augustine: Confessions and Enchiridion* (Philadelphia: Westminster Press, 1960), pp. 365, 399.

[4]The Augustinian position was held by the leading Roman Catholic theologians of the Middle Ages, including the authoritative St. Thomas Aquinas. It was also held by most of the leaders of the Protestant Reformation, including Martin Luther and especially John Calvin. The latter emphasized it so strongly that it is frequently coupled with his name.

Twentieth-century theologians of the Calvinist or "Reformed" tradition tend to allow some room for human free will. For instance, James Montgomery Boice in *God the Redeemer* (Downers Grove, Ill.: InterVarsity Press, 1978) states that we have personal choice in such matters as what profession to enter, what school to attend, what kind of food we will eat (pp. 46-47). But we do not have free will spiritually. Adam had it, but lost it in the Fall, and since then all women and men have been born into the state Adam was in consequent to the Fall.

Opposition to the Augustinian position is usually (and loosely) referred to as *Arminianism*. This stronger emphasis on the role of free will received impetus from the eighteenth-century Wesleyan revival. A vigorous recent criticism of St. Augustine is presented by Roger T. Forster and V. Paul Marston in their book entitled *God's Strategy in Human History* (Wheaton, Ill.: Tyndale, 1973). See especially pp. 257-88.

[5]Butterfield, p. 95.